St Paul the Hero

I0156116

TARSUS

ST PAUL
THE HERO

BY

Rufus M. Jones

DAWN CHORUS

San Rafael, Ca

Dawn Chorus Press, 2007
First edition, The Macmillan Company, 1923

For information, address:
Dawn Chorus Press, P.O. Box 151011
San Rafael, California 94915, USA

Library of Congress Cataloging-in-Publication Data

Jones, Rufus Matthew, 1863–1948.
St. Paul the hero / Rufus M. Jones.
p. cm.
Originally published: New York : Macmillan, 1917.
ISBN-13: 978-1-59731-350-6 (pbk. : alk. paper)
1. Paul, the Apostle, Saint—Juvenile literature.
2. Christian saints—Turkey—Tarsus—
Biography—Juvenile literature. I. Title.
BS2505.J67 2007
225.9′2—dc22
[B] 2007027562

CONTENTS

PICTURES AND MAPS

ST. PAUL THE HERO

ST. PAUL THE HERO

I

THE BOY OF TEN YEARS

"FATHER, who made the mountains that reach clear up into the sky over there where the sun goes down in the west?"

"It was God, my dear little boy. Don't you remember the psalm we read in the synagogue last week: 'I will lift up mine eyes unto the mountains, from whence cometh my help. My help cometh from the Lord who made the heavens and the earth'? God made the Taurus Mountains on the west of our dear city and He made those peaks of the Amanus you see off there in the East, over which the storks fly in the autumn, and He made this wonderful river, the Cydnus, which dashes through the cleft in the mountains and makes those great waterfalls which you love and which rushes headlong through the city on its way to the blue sea."

"Well, Father, He must be wonderful if He did that! But I don't see how He ever could spread out this great blue tent of a sky over all these fields and over all the city and over both the mountain ranges and as far as men have ever been. All the way to holy Jerusalem it goes — and farther, to Alexandria where the man lives, who wrote the book you read to me yesterday. Is there any end to that tent and what is it made of? Nobody in all our province of Cilicia can weave tent-cloth like that!"

"No, my son, nobody has ever found an end to the tent of the sky. It covers the whole world. It is harder to get to the end of it than it is to go to the end of the rainbow, which you tried to find a few days ago. But, my dear boy, God has made something more

FALLS OF THE CYDNUS

wonderful than the mountains, more wonderful than the river, more wonderful even than the blue canopy of the sky, that covers the world."

"What can it be, Father, that is more wonderful than these things? Do you mean the sea, which you sail over when you go as a pilgrim to holy Jerusalem, to the passover?"

"No, not the sea, though that *is* wonderful and dreadful. I mean the law which God wrote with His own finger and gave to our great prophet Moses. That is God's greatest gift to our race. I want my little boy to love the beauty of the mountains and the river and the sky and the sea. But beyond all things, I want him to love the holy law of God, to learn it by heart, to keep every word of it and to grow up and be one of Jehovah's own men. My boy comes of the tribe of Benjamin, the favourite of all the sons of our father Jacob, and some day this little boy may become the leader and deliverer of God's longsuffering people. Will little Saul promise to be Jehovah's man, and will he always love and keep the whole law which our God gave to Moses?"

"Will it be very hard to do, Father, and must I give up all the things I like to do?"

"Yes, my dear boy, it will often be very hard and you will have to give up some things you like to do. But if you keep the whole law of God and make yourself perfect and do everything God asks you to do in the holy law, all the people of our race forever will call you blessed, and you will be the hero of the tribe of Benjamin, and you will help to bring the Messiah for whom we long and pray, and Jehovah will give you eternal life in His kingdom."

"Oh, Father, I don't care how hard it is, I will do it. I will let my pet stork out of his cage, so that he can fly off with the other storks over the mountains. I will not do one

single thing on the holy Sabbath that is wrong.
I will not play by the river any more with
little Gentile boys.   I will learn every word of
Moses' law and say it all to mother when she
puts me to bed.   I will be ready to serve my
race when God calls for some one to do the
great deed, as David did in the book we
read."

His father patted his boy on the head and
smiled, as they walked home along the banks
of the rushing Cydnus and looked off at the
sun-lit tops of the Taurus Mountains.

Little Saul had had ten birth-days and he
had already caught the spirit of his race
which was very strong in his father and
mother who kept feeding him on the stories
of the past and waking in him the desire to be
the hero of his tribe.   Tarsus, a beautiful
city of the province of Cilicia, was his home.
The city was twelve miles from the Mediterranean Sea and ships came up the river to
the great wharves on either bank.   Not far

away to the south was the great island of Cyprus and through a pass in the Amanus Mountains a road went to Jerusalem and the land of his fathers. He had been often ill and weak during the ten years he had lived and often he had lain by the window and looked out on the world and wondered. More than once he had seen an army go marching up the street, carrying the Roman eagles and flashing Damascus blades in the sun. He wondered where they were going and what they would do with these terrible swords.

He had an older sister who was too old to play games with him, but she took him on walks by the river and like everybody else she told him Hebrew stories about the heroes he loved. She would picture to him often a city on a great hill, with valleys running round it, with a gorgeous temple in it, and she would say, "Some day you and I will go there to live and that will be our home and we shall be where we can see the temple of God every day!"

Saul's father was proud of many things. He had married a wise and beautiful woman, of his own tribe, who made his home a very happy one. He was proud of his wife. He was proud of this strange boy who pondered and wondered and who promised to become some day a great Rabbi and leader. He was proud of his tribe and of his race. He was still more proud to be a Pharisee and to be classed among those who strictly kept the law and worshipped every least letter of it, and then he was proud that he was a Roman citizen. He had done some service to the empire and the great honour of being enrolled a citizen had been conferred upon him, so that little Saul had been born a Roman citizen and had received a double name, one for his home people—Saul, and one for Roman citizens to call him by, Paul, which meant, "the little one."

This was the boy who talked with his father by the shore of the Cydnus, one evening about twenty years after Christ was born in Bethlehem.

II

MONTHS passed by and the little boy of
Tarsus grew stronger and more eager and
earnest. His father had sailed from the port
of Messina for Tyre and Ptolemais and Cæsarea, on his way to Jerusalem to keep the Passover in the Holy Land. Little Saul had
begged to be taken with him that he might
see the Temple and stand on the very ground
over which the great heroes of his race had
walked, but he was told that he must wait until he was a few years older and then he should
go to Jerusalem to study with a great Rabbi
who could answer all his questions. For a
long time he had gazed at the sky where the
sun had gone down over the Taurus. He was
really not looking at anything—he was just

gazing off into space and wondering. He wondered whether he would ever see the world beyond those mountains, the world he had heard men talk about, the world of Asia and Greece and Rome. Then he turned to look toward the dim, yet shimmering peaks in the East and he wondered whether he would some day climb those ranges and go through the pass into Syria and on into the land he loved best—the real world of his own race.

He had not yet read any of the stories of Greece. He had dimly heard of the Trojan war, but it was only a name of little meaning. Theseus and Jason and Achilles and Ulysses were not his heroes. They were never mentioned in his home, though he sometimes heard the boys in the street speak of them. *His* heroes had all lived over the other mountains. Their names he heard almost every day. They were household words. He sometimes made believe that he was David and he would run with a little hand sling and kill again the mighty Philistine giant that threatened his people. When he climbed a high hill-top he imagined himself Moses on Nebo, looking over Jordan on the wonderful land of promise, and every peak covered with a cloud that looked like smoke seemed to him once more Sinai, with the Lord above giving the law in the darkness and the thunder. He wished he could see the Seraphim as Isaiah did, with two wings over their faces, and two wings all the way down to their feet and two wings moving like a bird's to carry them wherever the Lord willed them to go. And still more he wished that he could see that wonderful figure which Ezekiel saw by the river Chebar—a living creature with the face of a man, and a calf and a lion and an eagle, all woven in and out with wings and all full of eyes, flashing like lightning, whirling like wheels, and moving wherever the Spirit of God carried the strange living creature. He thrilled whenever he heard the story of Daniel and he wondered whether he himself would have dared to pray to Jehovah and go to the lions for it. He had seen a lion once who was being carried to Ephesus in a cage, to be let out in the amphitheatre. The lion roared and shook his cage and showed his terrible teeth. Then little Saul thought of calm, brave Daniel going down into a den full of beasts like that.

And Shadrach, Meshach and Abed-nego, the three heroes of the burning fiery furnace, were men he loved to hear about. "Be it known unto thee O King, that we will not serve thy gods, nor worship the golden image which thou hast set up." Those words always stirred him like a trumpet. And he waited every time to hear once more about one like unto a son of God walking with these brave Jews in the midst of Nebuchadnezzar's fire. But best of all he liked the story of the faith of great father Abraham. He could almost see him laying the sticks of wood on the altar and binding his own only boy upon them. He wondered if *his* father would have done it with him, if *he* heard the Lord tell him to do it! Then suddenly came the joyous relief: the ram in the thicket, and little Isaac spared, just as the dreadful knife flashed in the air.

These heroes were going in procession through his mind as he gazed at the eastern gate in the mountains through which the road ran that led on toward the one city of all the world. Just then his mother stood by his side and took his hand in hers. She could see that big thoughts were moving in him and she felt a kind of awe as she looked down at the pale earnest face.

"Mother, which is the hardest of all the commandments to keep—I mean, really to keep, and not to break at all?"

In her mind, the fond Jewish mother standing in the dusk by the boy she loved, ran over all the commandments. "Thou shalt not have any other gods but Jehovah."

"Thou shalt not make any graven image."

"Thou shalt not take the name of the Lord thy God in vain."

"Thou shalt observe the Sabbath day and keep it holy."

"Thou shalt honour thy father and mother."

"Thou shalt do no murder."

"Thou shalt not commit adultery."

"Thou shalt not steal."

"Thou shalt not bear false witness."

"Thou shalt not covet, or desire." While she was thinking how to answer, little Saul said: "I know which is the easiest."

"And which is it?" asked his mother.

"Thou shalt honour thy father and mother. It is the easiest thing there is to do. I don't have to stop to think to do that! It is not so easy, though, to keep the Sabbath day holy. There are so many things to remember. Now that I have let my pet stork go, I do not feel tempted any more to play with him on the Sabbath day. But sometimes I start off for a walk before I think, and I carry things that are too heavy to be lifted on the Sabbath day. I wonder if I shall ever get so righteous, like our great Hebrew saints, that I shall not do anything wrong on the Sabbath day. It is very, very hard to be perfectly good. Do you not think, Mother, that this is the hardest of all the commandments to keep?"

"No, my dear Saul, there is one which you will find much harder to keep. It is the last one in the list: "Thou shalt not want things —thou shalt not desire." This commandment has to do with what goes on inside. All the others are about things we do in the world outside. This one is in there where you think. It says that you must rule your own spirit and not want or desire what you ought not to have or ought not to do. That my little boy, as he grows larger, will find very hard indeed to keep. Only the great God who guided Abraham our father all the way from Ur of the Chaldees to the dear land of Canaan can help my boy to keep that commandment."

"Anyway I shall try, mother. It isn't any harder is it than going into a den of lions or into Nebuchadnezzar's fiery furnace?"

"Ah, but my Saul will never have any such dreadful things to do, for he is born a Roman citizen and he can always appeal to Cæsar. Now it is time little boys were in bed."

III

IN JERUSALEM

THE days grew to weeks and the weeks to
months; the months added themselves and
made years in Tarsus in the first century just
as happens now where my young reader lives.
Time and the multiplication table go on in
one century exactly as in another, no matter
what else changes. Before the father and
mother could quite realise it, or believe it possible, Saul, once our little boy, who looked out
on his world and wondered, was old enough
to go away from his home to a great school in
Jerusalem where perhaps all his questions
could be answered though only for a little
while. His sister had married now and lived
in Jerusalem and it was arranged for Saul to
have his home with her while he was studying with the famous Rabbi Gamaliel, who

knew better than almost any one else the law,
and the rules by which the daily life of a strict
Jew should be guided so that he might be perfect.

Through the Syrian Gate in the Amanus
ridge, Saul had gone with his father on their
way to the holy city for the Passover and for
a short time of sight-seeing and visit before
the hard work of the school began. They
came on through Antioch of Syria, the first
great city which Saul had ever seen and one
which some day he would know much better;
then they journeyed on by hard and dangerous roads until they saw Damascus, with its
two beautiful rivers and its high city walls.
Some day Saul would know this city better
too! And the time would come when he
would find out how high those city walls
were! Every foot of the road from Damascus was crowded with interest and excitement
for this fifteen-year-old boy who was seeing
the holy land for the first time. Now he

thrilled in a new way as he actually saw with his eyes the scenes which before he had only pictured in imagination. When they crossed the Jordan, just south of the blue lake of Gennesareth, he could hardly contain himself. More than once he threw himself on the ground with his arms outspread as though he were trying to grasp the country and embrace it.

The road up from Jericho to Jerusalem was so dangerous and he had heard so many tales of robbers there that he was too frightened to enjoy the journey. But when at length *the city*—the city of all the world—with its shining temple gleaming in the sun came in sight, he forgot all about robbers and dangers and his sore and tired feet, and fell on his face and thanked God for letting him see the Holy City about which he had dreamed and imagined ever since he was a tiny boy. There it was! It was no dream but a real city, with real streets and walls and houses, and above all the temple, to his mind the holiest place in all the world.

The next day when he came to the temple, his heart beating and his throat swelling with emotion, he read with pride the inscription carved on the stones: "Only he that is a Jew may enter this sacred temple. If any one that is not a Jew enters he will be answerable for his death, which will ensue." Around him thronged a vast multitude of people who had come from all parts of the known world to be present on the Great Day of Atonement. He could see the choirs of singing men and he could hear the far-away sound of harps, and then he saw the long line of priests with their dress as Moses had described it in the books of the law and the high-priest with his gorgeous robe, and on his breast were the mysterious stones which no man understood save he who had them.

After the great days of the sacred week had passed and he had seen the wonders of the city,

Saul entered the cloister door and came into the sombre room where the learned doctor, Gamaliel, gathered his students at his feet to teach them. The boy was filled with awe as he got his first sight of the white-haired man who was to be his guide in the mysteries of the law and he made a deep salaam before him and remained bowed until the Master said: "Rise, my son, and be seated here."

The quick-eyed boy noticed at once that his new teacher was as full of kindness as he was of wisdom. There was something in the face of the old Rabbi that gave him confidence and dismissed his fear.

"Dost thou know the commandments?" asked the teacher.

"I know them all," answered the youth. "I have said them many times to my mother in Tarsus."

"Dost thou know what the law requires a faithful son of Abraham to do on the Sabbath day?"

The youth surprised his teacher as he ran through the long and complicated lists of things that a faithful Jew might do and might not do on the Sabbath day. At last the teacher stopped the boy and gravely asked, "where hast thou studied?"

"With my father and with my mother in the long evenings at Tarsus. My father is one of the wisest and one of the most strict of all the tribe of Benjamin and my mother is like the woman of whom the wise king Lemuel wrote in the Roll of Proverbs. They have taught me many things but I lack much and therefore have I come to Rabban Gamaliel."

"Canst thou recite the fifth book of Moses without a mistake?"

"I can recite every word duly, for the book itself says 'Lest ye forget.' "

"Thou hast done well, my son, and thou hast walked many steps in wisdom for one so young, but now thou must learn the *authorities*, thou must become skilful to interpret, thou must know the unwritten law and all the traditions of the Elders and Scribes and thou must fill thy mind with all the gathered wisdom of the great Rabbis until thou canst explain every passage in the Rolls of the books which Jehovah our God has given us through the holy men of old. Thou must work with diligence, beginning early in the morning and continuing so long as the light lasts, and thou must spend years here with me until thou hast won the truth and until thou knowest clearly what brings God's righteousness to a man. Art thou ready to give up the years of strong youth; art thou willing to lose the pleasures of the world; art thou able to endure the toil; wilt thou go all the way to the end with me?"

Saul stepped one step nearer, raised his fine face and his dark eyes full of eagerness to the master's face and calmly said: "Great Rabban, for that I come. I have left the things that are behind. I seek only one thing in this world—to be righteous, to know the whole secret of God, to be a perfect son of Abraham. Let it cost what it will, I follow where the wise Gamaliel shall take me, even to the end of the long road to truth."

Then the teacher bowed his head and prayed that the great Jehovah of the fathers would bless and enlighten the youth from Tarsus who was to be for many months in the cloister of Gamaliel.

IV

IN RABBI GAMALIEL'S SCHOOL

THE person who is a real hero in spirit and nature can be a hero at school as well as anywhere else. In fact those who prove to be heroes in later life are almost always heroes in their school-days. This youth who had come to Jerusalem from Tarsus of Cilicia did not have to wait for some occasion, with all the world looking on, before he could rise to heroic actions. He found a chance to be heroic even in the quiet uneventful cloisters of Gamaliel's school. All the boys and young men who gathered round this famous teacher very soon knew that a brave fellow and a real, born leader had joined their ranks. When a hard and difficult thing was to be done they turned naturally to him. When a question was asked which taxed everybody's brain, they all looked for him to answer.

There was no end to his zeal. Nothing seemed too hard for him. He had learned Greek as a boy in his home at Tarsus and he had always known the current Hebrew speech, but now he learned carefully the ancient Hebrew of his fathers. He pored over the Rolls of Scripture and took note of each jot and tittle. He learned all the fine points of grammar which his great Rabban could teach him. His patience seemed never to give out and he would work on in his search for truth long after the others had rolled up in their strange mat-like beds and were lost in peaceful slumber.

He seemed to think of ignorance as a great giant enemy to be fought with and to be killed, no matter how long and hard the fight might be. It was in this fight he showed his true heroic fibre. He was always hunting a new weapon to fight with, or he was sharpening an old weapon in his possession. He would travel miles to find a book he wanted or to discover what a strange word meant or to consult some authority whose opinion he desired.

"What do you suppose that Saul of Tarsus will be when he grows up?" the boys would ask of one another.

"He will surely be a great Rabbi and have a school in Jerusalem, like our master," one would say.

"I think he will be greater even than that," another would say. "I think sometimes, as I look at his face and watch him while he reads, that perhaps he will be a new prophet and bring a new word of God to our people."

"But that is not possible," a pious youth from a Jerusalem family would answer. "The words of God have already all been given. There will be nothing new until Messiah comes. I have heard my father say that many times."

This coming of Messiah was one of the
things our youth from Tarsus studied most
carefully. The books and traditions had
much to say about it, but it was hard to decide
just what would happen and just how to get
ready for this greatest event of all the world.
With the help of Gamaliel and his books,
young Saul came to believe that a great day
was soon to come for Jerusalem and for all
good Jews. A new king, like David, only
greater and wiser and better and stronger
would suddenly appear. He would have
power to turn stones to bread, or to leap from
the top of the temple to the ground without
being hurt in the least. He would break the
Roman army all to pieces in a minute. He
would call hosts of angel soldiers from the sky
at the sound of a trumpet and they would destroy or carry away all who had been bad Jews
and had not kept the law. Then he would
make Jerusalem a perfect city. The streets
would all be cleansed and purified, until one

could see his face reflected in every pavement.
The walls would be changed into precious
stones, the gates into pearls, and every person
left in the city would be as pure as the city itself. Nobody would be sick any more, nobody would die, or have any sorrow. And
best of all, all the good Jews who had ever
lived would be brought back to life again to
live in the perfect Jerusalem with the good
people who were there with the great king.
This king of their hopes and dreams was called
"Messiah," because he would be "anointed"
by God himself to rule forever. Saul believed that his people were the only ones out
of all the world who would have this king for
their king and this perfect city, and all who
had ever done anything against his nation
would suffer and suffer and suffer, while the
happy Jews were enjoying their beautiful
Mount Zion.

He believed, too, and he thought his books
proved it, that he and others who were willing

to work for it, could hurry up this great day and make it come sooner. This is the way you could do it. It couldn't come until there were a great many persons who were good enough to start the new world and the perfect city. The king, Messiah, would not come until he could find a large number of people all ready for him and as near perfect as you could be. Now to be perfect you must keep all the law and do everything that God commanded in the Old Testament and in the traditions of the Rabbis. If you broke one single commandment, it was as bad as though you broke them all, for if you broke *one,* then you had not kept the whole law.

Now my reader will see, I hope, what a hero this young Saul was. He had decided to be one of the men who would be ready for this mighty king and he was resolved to live the kind of life that would help bring him soon. He was going to live as though the perfect city had come already. He would not do one thing that would seem like disobeying God—even the littlest. Gamaliel had one student who was trying with all his might to be perfect, and that meant, to be a hero.

V

TENT-MAKING IN TARSUS

LIKE winged birds, the time flew by, just as it does now for school-boys and school-girls and Saul's years at the feet of Gamaliel were over. He had changed very much while he had been in Jerusalem. Soft hair was growing on his face now. His forehead was broader and fuller, but his shoulders were bowed over and he walked with a stoop because he had bent over his books so long and had taken very little exercise in these years of eager study. His hands were soft as a woman's and he seemed thin and worn with the strain of his thoughts. But the same fire was in his dark eyes and the same fine beautiful light shone on his face. He wondered as he came up the river Cydnus from Messina to Tarsus (for he returned by sea), whether his mother would know him. The news had spread that the boat was coming and the whole family in the home at Tarsus were on the watch for the returning scholar. He did not have much time to wonder whether his mother would know him, for he soon felt her arms around his neck and he found himself once more in the dear home with everybody looking him over and asking him questions until he needed three or four tongues to answer them all. His mother did not like the stoop in his shoulders but everything else pleased her. The father was too proud of his splendid son and too much moved with joy to say much, though he had already given a brief prayer of thanksgiving to Jehovah for the safe return, and for the wonderful gift of such a man-child as this. Meantime a servant was killing the fattest of all the full-grown kids for the feast of joy which all the household joined in preparing, and the whole day was given up to rejoicing.

It was a proud moment for the family the next Sabbath when young Saul was given the Roll of Scripture at the Synagogue and was asked to read the lesson and explain it. There he stood with all the Jewish families of Tarsus looking on and listening while he told them things they had never heard before. When the lesson was finished many a man turned to Saul's father and said: "God has given you a remarkable son. He will be an honour to our race and to our city."

Now the time had come when Saul's trade must be decided upon, for all young men who were to be Rabbis were expected to learn a trade, so that they could support themselves. Early and late in the home the question was discussed: What was the best trade for a slight, thin, soft-handed youth who was a great scholar and who was soon to be a famous teacher? The mother wanted him to learn a trade that would straighten his shoulders and make him strong and robust. The father thought he ought to select some occupation that would be refined and dignified and very honourable. After long and careful consideration, it was finally settled that Saul should learn the trade of weaving the goats' hair to make heavy tent-cloth and to cut the cloth into tent patterns and to sew the long tent seams.

It was strange work for the delicate scholar —so different from poring over books and settling points of the law. At first the soft hands blistered and the muscles were very tired with the work of the stiff hand-loom. But little by little the hands grew harder and the arms learned the trick of the motions and the work became natural and easy. Saul went at this work the way he did everything else. "It is," he would say, "a part of my life. I cannot succeed unless I can support myself and so I must make tents a little better than anybody else can do it. Some good stiff work now and the habit of doing every part of it right will make the whole thing easy for me later."

He went to the best maker of tents in the city and worked with him, for he knew the worth of a good teacher. But this teacher was so different from his old master in the school at Jerusalem! Like Gamaliel, this man also knew every fine point in his field of work. He had the secret of selecting the finest goats' hair and he knew the best weaves for making water-tight cloth and he drew the best patterns for both large tents and for small ones, and he had new ways of sewing seams that would neither rip in the wind nor leak in the hardest rains. The only trouble with him was that he was a Gentile and not a man of Saul's race. But he, too, was a scholar. He had studied in the great University of Tarsus and he knew many books which Saul had never read or even heard about. While they worked at the tent-cloth the master workman talked much to Saul of what he had learned in the University under his Stoic teachers, for Tarsus was one of the greatest centres of Stoic wisdom in all the world.

"Do you know," he would say, as they sat sewing the long seams, "all my books say that God is a great Spirit who fills all the universe, just the way the soul dwells in and fills the body. This Spirit is in the ocean and in the river, in the mountains and in the trees, in the air and in the cloud, in the stars and in the sun and above all it is in the mind of man. It makes everything full of purpose, and intelligent. The bee and the spider are wise because this Spirit dwells in them and teaches them. One of our own poets who lived here in Tarsus, in a great hymn to the Allwise One, says that we men of earth are children of God because our spirits have come from his Spirit, and this Spirit lives and moves in us, if we are good and wise. The human soul is like a little inlet into which the great sea flows. Bad and wicked men have become bad and wicked because they shut themselves off from the inflowing tides of that great divine Spirit. Those who have most of this divine Spirit in their souls do not fuss or worry. They are not disturbed over what happens to them. They say that the only thing that matters is to be master of your own spirit and not to be conquered by anything in the world. If I should lose all my goats and all my tent-cloth, and if all my looms should burn up, I could still be a brave man and start again just as though nothing had happened, but if I lost my spirit and began to whine and lament, nobody could cure me of that. Then I should be beaten and defeated. We Stoics try to be citizens, not only of our own city but of the whole world. We love our own people. We are proud of our own race, but we want more than that. We take an interest in all men everywhere. We want all cities to be good cities. We want all people everywhere to know God and love him, and we want to

make one great family on the earth, all living
in harmony under the great Spirit."

Saul stopped sewing and sat perfectly still.
It was different from anything he had heard
in Jerusalem. It could not be true or Gamaliel would have known it and yet it was so
wonderful and beautiful. He would think
about it more, and he would read some of the
books of the Stoics who said that we are the
offspring of God!

VI

THE GREAT TEACHER OF GALILEE

WHILE the young scholar was working at his new trade of weaving tent-cloth and making tents in the busy, thriving town of Tarsus, wonderful things were occurring beyond the Amanus Mountains, in the land of Palestine. Every traveller who came from Galilee and every pilgrim who passed through Capernaum brought tidings of a strange and extraordinary Teacher, totally unlike the great Rabbis and Scribes.

In far-away Tarsus not much was reported at first of what this Teacher said. The travellers told, first of all, of the wonderful things He did.

One man had heard, as he came through Galilee, of a little girl who had been very ill.

Nobody could help her. At last in despair the father went out to search for this Teacher, to see if He could do anything to save his daughter. He found Him by the lakeside preaching to a great multitude of people, and he begged Him to come at once, to make his daughter whole. Many strange and unusual things happened on the way and, at last, when they arrived, the little girl seemed beyond help, for she lay all still and did not breathe. But this remarkable Person took her by the hand and spoke some words in His own Hebrew language and the girl rose up and walked and was instantly well, and everybody wondered.

Many other such things they told of this Teacher. He made all kinds of sick people well. He even made totally blind persons see. All the towns around the Lake of Gennesareth were full of excitement over His cures and His other miraculous doings, and in all the country throughout Galilee people everywhere talked about Him and went long journeys to see Him, and to bring sick persons to Him.

Then, slowly, reports began to come of His words and His teachings. They said He seemed to have found out something new and strange about God. He was not afraid of God as other people were. He loved Him and talked about Him as though He knew Him. He kept calling God His Father, and He said God wanted to be Father to all persons, because He was full of love and tenderness for everybody in the world. He kept telling, in all His talks with the people who came to hear Him, about a new kingdom which He was trying to set up in the world. It was very hard to tell from the vague reports, which the travellers brought, what this kingdom was to be. It did not seem like the "new Jersualem," that Saul had learned about in Gamaliel's school. It seemed even greater than that, for it seemed like a new kind of

world for everybody.   Everybody, who loved
God and learned how to live a life of love
and kindness to all people everywhere, could
be in it, and it would grow and spread like
seeds of grain in the field.

Then, later, when the people who had gone
up from Tarsus to the Passover, came back
from Jerusalem, they brought news of a terrible thing that had happened there during
the Passover week. This Teacher, it would
seem, had come up to keep the Passover and
the common people had discovered Him and
they thought at first that He must be the long-
expected Messiah and they had made a procession for Him and had tried to proclaim
Him their king. But this and other things
frightened the rulers in Jerusalem and they
sent by night and seized Him and got Pilate,
the governor of Palestine, to condemn Him
and crucify Him. Then all the people turned
against Him and thronged out of the city in
great multitudes to see Him nailed on the

cross and to see Him die hanging in the air.
And the pilgrim who brought the reports
said He was not like any other victim that
was ever crucified. Instead of shouting and
wailing and cursing, He had been calm and
unmoved. Every time He spoke, His words
were full of love. Once He spoke in a quiet,
gentle way to a thief who was crucified on a
cross near Him. And once, and this was the
strangest thing they reported, He looked up
toward the sky and then out toward the great
multitude of shouting people and said in a
gentle voice which reached out over all the
throng, "Father, forgive these people. They
do not know what they are doing."

A few who came back later had another
story which they told but they couldn't make
anybody at Tarsus believe it. They said that
some of the followers and friends of this wonderful Teacher from Galilee declared that
they had seen Him alive after He was crucified. Some of these followers said they had

heard Him speak just the way He used to do before He was crucified, and they claimed that He told them when they were on the way going up to Jerusalem that He would be crucified, but that He would come back to life again.

When Saul heard these strange reports he was at first very much moved by them. He could not sleep at night because he thought so much over the stories he heard from the travellers. But little by little he made up his mind that they were just idle tales such as travellers love to tell to those who stay at home. He said to himself: "It isn't likely that there really was any such person in Galilee as this one they tell about. I should have heard about him while I was in Jerusalem, for he could not have got his power suddenly and if he was beginning to do these wonderful things then, it would have been known in the city. But nobody had heard of him at all. If he got his power suddenly, without any preparation and without studying in any of the schools, it is probable that some evil spirit, like Beelzebub, has helped him and revealed secrets to him. It is almost certain that he was not sent by God, for the books of the law do not tell about any such Teacher who would come and die for his truth, and the words they bring about his teaching are not at all like what we know of God from our sacred books. No, either there was no such person, or, if there was, he was deluded and misguided."

But when Saul was talking one beautiful evening with his mother, who seemed now much older than when. she talked about the commandments with her little boy, suddenly Saul said: "Wouldn't it be strange, Mother, if what that Galilean Teacher, of whom the travellers talk, said about God were really true—I mean, that God is a Father and loves men, even men who do wrong and sin. My tent-maker thinks that God is a great Spirit who dwells in everything and is everywhere.

But *this* is more wonderful, that God is full of love and tenderness for all kinds of people in the world. It cannot, however, be true, for the Rabbis would have known it if it had been so!"

And the mother answered: "Ah, yes, no doubt the wise Rabbis would know. But is there not something just a little like that in some of the beautiful psalms which we sing in the Synagogue—'Like as a Father'?"

"But, Mother, this man, they say, died on a cross, and no good man, whom God approved, could die that way, for our law says that all who are hanged on trees are cursed and disapproved of by God, so that we need not think any more about him." But try as he would, Saul could not get these things out of his mind.

VII

IN JERUSALEM AGAIN

ALL through the quiet period in Tarsus while Saul was learning his trade and living with his father and mother in the dear old home where he had been a boy, he was wondering what his life was going to be. He always felt, even as a little boy, that a great life-work lay before him. It was too sacred and solemn to talk about and he did not tell even his mother, but all the time, down deep in his soul, he dimly knew that he was destined to have an unusual life and to do something signal and wonderful. When he lay ill and everybody thought he would die, he felt very sure that he was not going to die yet, for the great work of his life was still to be done! He had often been in great danger, on his

journey up to Jerusalem and on the ship coming back to Tarsus, and many times before he
left home, but he always knew that somehow
he would come through the danger and be
spared.

He was eager now to find his life-work and
to start in on his great career.   He was, therefore, very happy when a traveller of his own
race, coming from the holy land, brought
him a letter from the authorities in Jerusalem
saying that they had work for him to do in
that city.   They wanted a young and learned
Rabbi to teach the Jews living in Jerusalem
who spoke Greek and who were called "Hellenists."   There were, my readers must know,
two kinds of Jews.   There were the Jews,
first, who lived all the time in Palestine.
They could keep the law more perfectly and
more completely than other people could.
They thought of themselves as the truly real
Jews and as the inner circle of God's own people.   Then, secondly, there were the Jews

who lived and did business in the great cities
of the Roman Empire—cities like Rome and
Alexandria, and Ephesus and Antioch and
Philippi and Corinth and Tarsus. They
could not keep themselves as pure or as perfect as the Palestine Jews could, for they had
to meet and mingle with Gentiles who were
not pure according to the law and who defiled
those that came in contact with them. Then,
too, these out-dwellers could not get to the
temple very often to make sacrifices and to
keep the requirements of the law. They used
the language which the worldly people around
them used. That was generally Greek.
They had their Scriptures translated into
Greek and many of them did not know and
could not read Hebrew at all. But these Hellenists, or Greek-speaking Jews, went up to
Jerusalem as often as they could and when it
was possible for them to do so, they would
stay in Jerusalem for long periods in order to
be near the temple. They had a synagogue of

their own in Jerusalem where they went for
their lessons and for their Sabbath services
and where their little children were taught
while the parents were staying in Jerusalem.
It was to this Synagogue that Saul, the young
Rabbi, was to go, to teach the Jews who came
from all the far-away countries to sojourn in
Jerusalem.

It was very different for him, going to
Jerusalem now from what it had been for the
fifteen-year-old boy the first time he went.
Now he was going, not for a few years, but for
life. Now he was setting his hand to carry
out the great dreams and hopes of his life.
Now he was leaving his mother, perhaps for
the last time. His father would still continue
to go to the Passover and Saul would perhaps
see him there, but his mother would never
leave home again and it would surely be many
years before he would come back through the
mountain-gate, or up the Cydnus River, to his
birth-place. Nobody knows just what goes

on in a young man's heart when he takes this great venture and pushes out from the home he loves to begin his real life in the strange and difficult world, where some succeed and where some fail, where some keep pure and good, and where some go wrong.

Many things seemed to have changed in Jerusalem during the short period since Saul had left it. Everybody was talking of the strange events that had taken place recently. A new people had appeared in the city. They called themselves "the people of the way," or "those of the way," or "those of Jesus' way." Others called them "Galileans," or "Nazarenes." They were men and women who believed that Jesus the great Teacher of Galilee was the Messiah and they declared that He was still alive and would soon return to be king and lord. They were growing fast in numbers and spreading in every part of the city. They met every day from house to house and ate their evening meal together in great joy and fellowship. They took care of all their poor people and their sick and they shared everything they had with one another as though they were all brothers and belonged to one great family.

The rulers in Jerusalem, however, did not like to see them spreading through the city. They watched them carefully and arrested the leaders when they found them doing anything to attract attention or trying to get others to join them. They did not like to be told that the person they had Pilate crucify was the Messiah, or that He was raised from the dead and was now alive. It was easy to see that there was sure to be trouble in Jerusalem, if these people went on increasing and if they would not keep quiet.

There were some of "those of the way" in the Synagogue where Saul was to be Rabbi. They were always ready to talk about their wonderful Teacher, who had been crucified and they were eager to prove that He was the real Messiah that had been so long expected. Saul thought he could very soon teach them sense and show them how foolish they were. He would quickly prove to them that Jesus could not be the Messiah, for the Messiah would surely never be crucified! He would come in splendour and glory, and if the Romans tried to crucify Him He would call down from heaven an army of angels and destroy all His enemies in a moment! And He would break the Roman Empire all to pieces, as one breaks an old jar of pottery. It would be only a few days, Saul felt sure, when he would be able to stop all this talk about a crucified Messiah. He would argue them down and make them ashamed to say such things any more. But Saul did not know how hard his task really was. He was to discover that some things in this world cannot be hushed up, or argued down!

VIII

THE MAN WITH A SHINING FACE

THERE was one man in this Synagogue of
the Hellenists more remarkable than any of
the other people who belonged to it. His
name was Stephen. I do not know what city
he came from. But he was one of the "out-
dwellers," and he had become a follower of
Jesus, "one of the way"—"a Nazarene." He
was different from any of the other followers
of Jesus. He saw farther than the rest did.
He seems to have been the first of "those of
the way" to realise that Jesus did not come to
be the Messiah of the Jews alone and to purify
their customs. Stephen thought He came to
bring life and light and joy to *all* the world.
The other followers of Jesus in this early
period were loyal, devoted Jews. They went
every day to the temple and they kept the law

as the other Jews did. They supposed that
Jesus was to be the king in Jerusalem and that
only Jews were to be His people. Those
who were not Jews could have no share in the
good news which He proclaimed.

Stephen was so pure and good and wise that
he got a new idea of what the coming of Jesus
meant. The truth was far bigger than the
others dreamed, and he began to see it, and to
tell about it. If God is Father, as Jesus kept
saying He was, then He must love all men as
well as Jews, and if God is Life and Spirit,
then He can come into men's lives everywhere
without any temple and without priests and
sacrifices. Stephen began to wonder, as he
thought about all that Jesus had said and
taught and done, whether His message was
not far greater and more wonderful even than
the law of Moses, whether some day it would
not take the place of the old system of laws
and customs and sacrifices and whether even
the temple itself might no longer be needed to

worship God in, for men might worship Him
anywhere where they happened to be.

Stephen was so bold and fearless, and he
was so full of his great idea, that he tried to
tell the people in Saul's Synagogue about it.
They all turned upon him and called him a
dangerous man. They tried to make him see
that he was not true to the religion of his
fathers, that he was teaching new ideas, that
he was turning people away from the old customs, and that if the people followed his
teaching they would overthrow the whole
wonderful system of Moses, and so make it
impossible for the Messiah to come, for
whom all good Jews were waiting and longing.

Saul, with all his learning and his knowledge, thought he could easily answer Stephen
and prove that he was entirely wrong. But
every time he tried, Stephen got the best
of him. Saul would quote texts from the
Old Testament and Stephen would rise up

and show that these texts meant something quite different from what Saul had always thought they meant. He was so powerful and his life was so noble that all the people who listened felt that even if he was wrong in his ideas he was great in his soul, and they began to wonder if he perhaps might be right and Saul wrong. Day after day the discussion went on without any end to it. At last Saul decided that this would never do. Some way must be found to stop this dangerous man who was leading the members of his Synagogue astray. He told the rulers in Jerusalem that he had discovered a traitor who must be arrested. "He talks against Moses," he said. "He does not love our holy land, or our holy law, or our holy temple, the way all true Jews should." Then the Council in Jerusalem had Stephen arrested and brought before them for trial, and witnesses came in and told all the things they could think of to make the Council condemn him.

While they were talking against him they all saw a light shine on his face, and he looked more like an angel than like an ordinary man, and everybody wondered what he would say in answer to the charges that were made against him.   And Saul must have been eager to see what was going to happen to this man with the shining face, whom nobody could defeat in an argument.   Then quietly Stephen began to speak for himself.   He did not try to prove that the things which had been said against him were false.   He paid no attention to his own case.   He told the Council that all through the history of their Hebrew race the people had always failed to see new light when God brought it to them; they had always missed the path when God was trying to lead them into a new way, and they had always misunderstood when God was trying to teach them new ideas. They cried out against Moses, he told them, in the wilderness. They worshipped a golden calf just at the time when he was giving them the law of God, and when the prophets came to teach them more about God, they served Moloch and other false gods instead of Him. Their great, wise king Solomon had told them, when he built the temple, that no temple, however wonderful, could contain the great God who fills the universe, but the people did not understand his words and seemed to think that God lived only in their temple. "You have always failed to see the truth," Stephen cried. "You have always persecuted prophets when God has sent them to you. You have killed those who told about the coming of Jesus. And now *you, yourselves,* have betrayed and killed Him when He did come. You talk about the law and you say that God gave it through angels. But you do not understand it and you do not really keep it."

That was more than they could stand. They forgot that they were judges and were having an orderly trial. They all rushed at

Stephen. They showed their teeth at him and howled him down. But he was as calm and steady as though everything were peaceful. In the midst of the uproar, they suddenly heard him say: "I see Jesus! There He is, up there in the open sky, at the right of God in His glory." Then they all stopped their ears, so that they might not hear what he said, and they rushed at him and dragged him out of the city and stoned him. As the people who stoned him pulled off their garments so that they could throw the stones better, they gave their garments to Saul to hold. He did not join in throwing the stones, but he approved of what the others were doing and he ran along with them and carried the garments. And he could see Stephen's wonderful face which was shining more than ever now! He did not say one hard word against those who were killing him. But just at the end, Saul heard him say: "Lord Jesus, do not blame these people for what they are doing"—"Wilt thou now receive my spirit to Thyself."   And then, with the stones raining round him, the brave, good Stephen died—with the light still on his face.

Saul never forgot that face. He thought Stephen was wrong and he believed that he must be stopped or he would bring harm to God's people. But he had never seen anybody die like that before! And the more he meditated and thought about it, the more he wondered at what Stephen had said, and still more over his dying words and his happy, shining face!

IX

THIS young man who now unexpectedly found himself a persecutor was by nature kind and tender-hearted. He had never wilfully hurt any creature or given pain to anybody. He had come up to Jerusalem for his life-career with the highest hopes and the noblest aspirations. His whole being was aflame with a passion for his nation. Ever since he was old enough to know the story of his own people he had dreamed of the splendid future that was soon to dawn. All that the greatest prophets had seen in distant vision, he believed he should one day see with his own eyes. He had tried, with almost superhuman effort, to make his own life perfect so that he might be one of the little inner circle of perfect

Jews, who would help to bring the Messiah and the perfect age and who would be ready for this glorious king when he should come.

Now he suddenly found, in his own Synagogue even, people who said that the Messiah *had come already,* that the rulers and Pharisees who were expecting Him and preparing for Him had not recognised Him when He did come and had crucified Him. This seemed to Saul an awful idea—an unbelievable tale. He was sure the Messiah could not be crucified. But he was afraid that these enthusiastic and misguided followers of Jesus would ruin his hopes. Everything that could be done must be done at once to stop their teaching and to destroy their influence. He saw only one way to guard the hope of Israel and that was to crush this movement absolutely and to shut up or kill every person who went about claiming that Jesus was the Messiah. It was a very disagreeable task, but it must be done for the good of the nation

and, however hard and distasteful it might
be, Saul was resolved to carry it through and
to leave nobody who would ever again dare
to say that Jesus, the crucified, was the long-
expected king.

Into the peaceful homes of the "Nazarenes"
he went and seized both men and women and
carried them away to prison.   He had to separate husbands from their wives.   He had to
take mothers away from their tender little
babies.   He had to break up meetings and
drag away those who were preaching the new
gospel to their eager listeners.   But everywhere he went he found that these people had
something which he did not have.   In the
midst of their sufferings and their trials they
were calm and peaceful and happy and trium-
phant and radiant.   When they were persecuted their faces shone with a light that
seemed almost heavenly.   They prayed for
those who injured them and were not disturbed by any troubles.   They kept saying

most remarkable words about Jesus and their faith in Him, and they all seemed to believe that He was still alive and that they would all soon be with Him.

Saul had been trying all his life to be perfect, to be fully righteous. He had worked with all his might to keep all the law and all the commandments. But he knew deep down in his soul that he had failed to reach his aim. He could not do it. He found something in himself which he could not govern. If he didn't break one commandment, he broke another. If he was strong at one point he was sure to be weak at another. That commandment which his mother had told him was the hardest to keep—"thou shalt not covet or desire"—was always bothering him. Even when he did not actually *do* wrong things, he found himself *wanting* to do them, and *that* he knew was wrong. It all filled him with discouragement, and sometimes with despair.

But these people whom he was persecuting

and dragging away to prisons seemed to be
good almost without trying.   They had found
a new power somewhere that seemed to help
them.   It made him wonder whether they
were perhaps right and he possibly was
wrong.   He hated what he was doing.   How
gladly he would stop it, if only he could be
sure that God did not want him to persecute
these strange followers of Jesus.   But until
God should make it perfectly plain to him, he
must go on with his hard duty.

He had heard of some of these "Jesus-peo-
ple" in the city of Damascus.   He would go
to that city and stop them before they had
time to spread.   He got documents from the
rulers in Jerusalem giving him power to ride
to Damascus and to seize these people and to
treat them as he had treated those in Jerusalem.   With his band of helpers he started off
on his journey, looking bold and fearless in his
face, but feeling in his soul that it was the
most disagreeable journey he had ever set out

upon, and wishing all the time that he could ride straight on through Damascus and the Syrian gate in the mountains to Tarsus, and give up the whole sorry work of dragging mothers away from their children. As he rode he thought and wondered.

The road took him through Capernaum and around the magnificent lake where Jesus had done much of His work, where He had preached His divine messages and where He healed multitudes of people. Saul could hardly stay at any inn in that country without hearing some wonderful story of the Galilean Teacher. He might easily see the father of the little girl who had been raised from her bed by this Teacher. He might talk with a man whose eyes had been opened, or with a person who had been delivered from leprosy or insanity, which the people in that day called being "possessed with devils." He might hear men tell how they themselves had heard this wonderful Galilean talk about God His

Father and about the kingdom of life and love. And he might hear strange stories of what had happened after the crucifixion—how fishermen who had lived by that lake all their lives had seen Jesus in glorified form, after He had been dead and buried.

Saul would ride on from Galilee with new thoughts surging in his mind. The simple faith of those who saw with their own eyes and heard with their own ears would stir him with fresh meditation as he rode over the stretch of country between Gennesareth and Damascus.

One thing had always made it impossible for him to believe that Jesus was divine, that He was sent by God or that He was the long-looked for Messiah: *He had suffered and died on the cross.* Saul felt sure that, if God had sent Him and He had been divine, He would not have had to suffer, but He would have come in glory and power. But as he rode along in silence and in deep thought, he remembered that he had heard these followers of Jesus say in their meetings that the Old Testament was full of prophecies which said that Christ must suffer. He began to think more carefully about these passages—especially the one in the fifty-third chapter of Isaiah: "He was despised and rejected of men; a man of sorrow and acquainted with grief." "Surely he has borne our griefs and carried our sorrows." "He was wounded for our transgressions, he was bruised for our iniquities." "As a lamb that is led to the slaughter and as a sheep that before her shearers is dumb; yea he opened not his mouth." "For the transgression of my people was he smitten." "He poured out his soul unto death and was counted with the transgressors, yet he bore the sins of many."

This might mean that God's great servant would not be glorious and full of power when He came but a sufferer. It might be that He would come and suffer for the sins of others, and that He would do for men what they could not do for themselves. He might be the perfect one and He might through His suffering and death bring them a new power to live by. If he was only sure that God had raised Him from the dead and had brought Him triumphantly through His sufferings and His crucifixion, then he could believe that this Galilean was the Saviour and the divine Deliverer for whom they had been waiting.

Stephen had cried out in his dying moments, "I see Jesus there, at the right hand of God." Saul had heard how others claimed that they had seen Him alive and glorified. He would be likely to say to himself as he rode along: "If *I* could only see Him as these others say they have done, I would believe as they do. I would stop this miserable work I am doing and I would follow Him forever and I would make everybody believe in Him."

Then in the stillness there suddenly broke

in upon this young man a light which seemed brighter than the mid-day sun in the sky and he saw Jesus and heard Him speak and call him and his whole life was forever changed by this wonderful thing that happened on the road to Damascus.

X

IN ARABIA

THOUGH dazed and blinded by the light, which seemed to come from another world beyond this world, Saul nevertheless felt perfectly sure that he *saw* Jesus glorified. Through all the rest of his life, he always said that he had *seen* Christ—he had seen Him as Stephen saw Him. He had seen Him as Peter and James and John saw Him and he never had any doubt any more that He was alive and victorious over death. He had heard Him speak, too, in that wonderful meeting outside the gate of the city. He had heard Him say: "I am Jesus whom thou persecutest." "Why persecutest thou *me?*"

All the rest of the way into Damascus, he walked in darkness. His outer eyes were still

blind from the light, but in the city his sight
came back again and he could see once more.
He knew that a mighty change had come
within himself, but he did not know at once
all that it meant. He wanted to go far away
from all the old scenes of his life, far away
from everybody he knew, far away from the
noisy, busy world, and think out what had
happened. Even before talking with Peter
and the other disciples of Jesus, he wished to
meditate alone and find his bearing in the new
experience which had so suddenly come to
him.

The greatest leaders of Saul's race had
found out the meaning of life, alone with God,
in the wilderness, or in the mountains, or on
the edge of the desert. Moses had come face
to face with God on Mount Sinai. Elijah
had heard the still small voice speaking to
him, far away from the rush and din of the
world. John the Baptist got his preparation
for his mission in the solitary wilderness un-

disturbed by people. Jesus had discovered in the desert how to come forth victorious over temptation and here he had realised that His kingdom was not to rest on force and worldly power. So, too, Saul now felt that he must go away from the city and live for a time in the heart of nature and open his soul to God.

He decided to go to Arabia for his period of quiet and of meditation. Perhaps he went, as Moses had gone, to Sinai, or to some other region of this strange, mysterious land of wilderness, mountains and deserts. He has not told us a word about his life in Arabia and none of his friends has given us any reports of these months of solitude and meditation. To-day, if any man wished to prepare for a great career of ministry or missionary service, he would go to some college or university or seminary or training school and learn how to do the work which lay before him, and he would train his body with games of skill and athletic courses, so as to be at his

very best in mind and heart and body.   Saul
had nothing of this sort open to him.   He had
finished his years of study but they only pre-
pared him to be a Jewish Rabbi, a teacher of
the law.   Now he wanted to learn how to tell
the world the full message, the good news,
which Jesus had brought to men.   There was
no school where this was taught.   There were
no Christian colleges or universities or semi-
naries yet.   There were only a few followers
of Jesus.   Most of them lived in Jerusalem,
and they were ignorant people—fishermen,
and tax-collectors—who had had no chance
to study.   The best thing Saul could do was,
therefore, to go away alone and read and think
and let God teach him.

At first he supposed that the good news
which Jesus had brought was for his own
people alone but as he meditated and studied
and listened he began to see that God's love
reached everybody and that the great Galilean
had come to bring new life to all people in the

world. It was many years perhaps before
Saul fully realised all that this meant, but I
think he began to see it in Arabia. Another
thing kept coming before him all the time.
He was eager to find out why Jesus had died
on the cross, why He had suffered, and what
it all meant. That also took years of thought
before he understood it, but here in the quiet of
the mountains he began to *see*. How we wish
he had written some letters from Arabia and
told what he was doing and thinking! If he
had only written to his mother once a week, or
even once a month, and she had preserved the
letters, how eagerly we would read them now!
But there is not a word about it all. We only
know that in the stillness his spirit was gathering power and his soul was growing richer.

At last he felt that he was "ready." This
is one of his great words—"I am now ready."
The time of quiet was over and the busy life
must begin. He felt sure he could make
everybody believe in his Christ. It was all so

plain and wonderful that people would be bound to listen as he told them what he had seen and known and felt! He decided to go back to Damascus and begin there—near the place where he had first seen Jesus and where the great change in his life had come.

But it was not as easy as he expected. In the first place he soon discovered that he needed to know more about the life of Jesus. He had not talked with anybody yet who had been with Him in Galilee and in Jerusalem. He must learn more about Him before he could move people with his words. And then he found that the people did not want to hear about Jesus. The Jews in Damascus all thought Saul was a traitor. He had started for their city to persecute the followers of Jesus and now he was one of the followers himself, trying to make them believe. They decided to seize him and do to him what he used to do to the followers of Jesus. They would soon put him where he would not talk any more about this Galilean Teacher. They watched all the gates of the city so that Saul could not get away and they had men hunting for him through the streets. But some of Saul's friends put him in a great basket and in the dark of the night, by a long rope, they let him down the side of the wall and he got far away from the dangerous city before the morning sun came up.

He must have felt a strange thrill as he passed by the place where he saw the great light and heard the voice saying: "Saul, why persecutest thou me?" But he hurried on over the road through Galilee and came to Jerusalem, which he had left three years before. He had started out a persecutor. He came back a follower of Jesus. He had crossed the "great divide."

XI

FIFTEEN WONDERFUL DAYS

WE have invented a little instrument called a "dictaphone." If one of these instruments is hidden away in a room, a person at the other end of the dictaphone can overhear all the conversation that goes on in the room where it is concealed, and the entire conversation can be written down and kept. How we wish now that there had been a dictaphone in the room in which Saul staid with St. Peter for fifteen days in Jerusalem. Part of the time James, the brother of Jesus, was there, too, with them. But the rest of the time they were alone—talking, talking, talking. St. Peter was telling Saul the things he wanted to know about the life of Jesus and about His death and resurrection. What a wonderful

story it would be, if we could only get it all
back, word for word! There was that keen
and eager face of the man still young, with all
his life-work before him, and opposite the
older man whose whole life had been boating
and fishing until one with authority had said
to him, "Follow me." The older man knew
more about this Galilean life than anybody
else knew, unless it were that other fisherman,
named John, and he could answer all the
questions the young man asked so long as they
were just questions about events, for he had
seen with his eyes and he had heard with his
ears and he had handled with his hands and he
knew.

The pity of it is, not a word of this conversation has been preserved. We can im-
agine what some of the questions were and we
can guess what some of the answers would be,
but the actual words are gone. They are lost
forever. What we do know, however, is
that at the end of these fifteen days of wonder-

ful talk, Saul went away from Jerusalem, his mind stored with truth about Jesus. He had heard from Peter's lips the supreme facts about the life of the Person who was henceforth to be Lord and Master of his own life. Peter and James told all their friends in Jerusalem what had happened to Saul, how his career had suddenly changed, how the man who once dragged harmless Christians to prison was now getting ready to give his whole life to the work of telling the good news about Jesus and they already saw that a mighty champion of the truth had joined them and they all thanked God for Saul of Tarsus. When he left Jerusalem, after his memorable visit with Peter, Saul probably went home to Tarsus, and he lived and worked for a time in the home province of Cilicia. There is a long period of his life at this time about which we know nothing at all. He must have been at work for he could not settle down and rest. There was a tremendous drive in his glowing spirit, and wherever he was something was always happening. If he spent some years in Tarsus, as is probable, it is certain that many people there heard of Jesus from him and we can well believe that he went from town to town through the mountain province to tell in all the synagogues the truth which he had learned.

It is possible, however, that he may at this time have had a long period of serious illness. He has himself given us one single glimpse into this unknown period of his life. In the twelfth chapter of Second Corinthians, he says that a tremendous experience came to him fourteen years before—that would be in this period. He was suddenly "caught up" into a higher world where he saw what nobody can see with ordinary eyes and where he understood the mysteries of life in a new way. It seemed for a moment as though he had lost his body and found his soul, as though he had leaped across all the space of the universe and

had come to God's dwelling-place and everything lay plain and clear before him. But
about this time, he says further, some terrible
illness came upon him, which was so bad that
it felt like "a thorn," or "a stake in his body"
—a piercing, racking pain that seemed to bore
into his quivering flesh. It was almost more
than he could endure. He begged and be-
sought that he might be relieved of it but it
lasted on and on. We do not know certainly
what this painful disease was but perhaps a
little later, as we go on with his life, we may
get some idea of what it was, for it appears to
have come back again when he was in Galatia.

What we do know is that, while he was
living in Tarsus, a man named Barnabas
thought of Saul and came to Tarsus to find
him. Barnabas was another man something
like Stephen. He saw farther than most of
the others did. He was always ready for new
things and he was full of faith and activity.
Like Saul, he could not rest—he wanted to tell

everybody what he had discovered. He heard of a new movement in the great city of Antioch, the capital of the province of Syria, and he went off to Antioch to see what this movement really was. When he got there he found that some followers of Jesus who had been forced to leave Jerusalem, because of the persecutions, had come to Antioch and had begun a little church there and were preaching to everybody who would listen. It did not make any difference to them whether the people who came to hear were Jews or not. They were as ready to tell the good news about Christ to Greeks as to the people of their own race. It was the first time and the first place in all the world that anybody had done this. In Jerusalem, "those of the way" were all Jews and they had nothing to do with anybody else. They never dreamed that peoples of all races were alike and were equally dear to God and that Christ came to bless and save all men. They made a sharp distinction be-

tween Jews and Gentiles. But in Antioch it
was all different. Those who formed the
church in Antioch forgot about race and
thought only about brotherhood. Greeks
flocked into the same room with Jews and
together they worshipped God like brothers.
And here in Antioch where this new spirit was
born and where this new movement began, the
followers of Christ were for the first time
called "Christians." In Jerusalem this word
was not used or thought of, because no outside
people came in and there was no need of a new
name. But in Antioch where the Greeks
joined the movement and where everybody
discovered that a new religion was born they
needed a word to name it with and so they
called these persons who talked so much
about Christ, "Christians." Barnabas was
filled with joy when he found what
was going on in Antioch. It looked like
the beginning of a movement that would sweep
across the world and change the whole em-

pire. He saw at once that he must have the best man whom he could find to help him push the work along, and as he sat thinking of the different persons who could do this great work, suddenly he remembered the young man whose persecutions had driven these first Christians to Antioch and he knew that Saul was now a changed man and a powerful champion of the truth. Whereupon he hurried off through the Syrian gate in the mountains to fetch Saul to Antioch and Saul went back with him to begin the greatest work any man has ever done in the world.

XII

THE FIRST GREAT MISSIONARY JOURNEY

ANTIOCH, the great Syrian city, from this time on became Saul's new home. He was henceforth to be very closely connected with the flourishing capital of Syria. This was now to be the mother-church of all his activities. From Antioch he started out on all his missionary journeys and he came back to Antioch at the end of each of his far-reaching travels. Here were faithful Christians praying for him as he worked and suffered and here, when he arrived weary and worn with labour, were dear friends to welcome him and to refresh him. Antioch was the first city in the world to have Gentile Christians in it and it was from this city that Christianity spread out over the world and con-

ANTIOCH

quered the Roman Empire and became a
world movement, and, as we shall see, the man
from Tarsus was in this great undertaking the
foremost leader and the untiring worker.

For a whole year Barnabas and Saul
worked in the city of Antioch, spreading the
knowledge of Christ through that region,
gathering in new people all the time, teaching
them the truth and helping them to live the
new way.   It was joyous work and while they
were doing it they were constantly discovering fresh light and were learning all the time
how to tell the world their "good news" and
how to build churches out of people who had
before been heathen and idol-worshippers.
At the end of the first year when the Antioch
church had become strong and vigorous—full
of life and power—Barnabas and Saul decided, with the approval of the entire church,
to go out and tell their message to the great
world around them.   They felt sure that God
called them to be missionaries and they re-

solved to go wherever He wanted them to go
and to do whatever they felt in their hearts
that He wanted them to do. These two men
took with them as their companion and helper
a third man, named John Mark, who had come
from Jerusalem to Antioch and who was
Barnabas' nephew. It was probably this
young man who later in life wrote the wonderful book which we call "The Gospel according to Mark."

The whole church came together for a very
solemn meeting and prayed for the travellers
and then the three men, full of joy and en-
thusiasm, set out on their journey down the
river to Selucia, where they took ship for the
island of Cyprus which lies west of the Syrian
coast. They visited all the cities of the island,
going from the eastern end across to the
western edge, to the city of Paphos where the
governor of the island lived. This governor
was greatly impressed with the message and
the extraordinary power of the missionaries

and he, Roman as he was, believed the wonderful new truths which they told him about God and about the Christ who had come to reveal Him.

From Paphos the little band of travellers struck out for a new field of work. They had been so successful in Cyprus that they now decided to attack a still larger and more difficult region of the earth. They sailed almost north from Paphos, to the shores of the Mediterranean, lying west of the Taurus mountains over which Saul gazed as a boy. They landed in the district of Pamphilia and came to the city of Perga, a little way in from the Sea. From this time on, our hero is never called Saul any more. His name suddenly changes here to Paul. It is probably due to the fact that the field of his work is now widening out to the Gentile world. He is leaving behind the narrow circle of his own people who always called him by his Jewish name and he is going out among the Greeks who henceforth call him by his Greek name, that has become so familiar to us.

Three things that concern our story seem to have happened at Perga. Paul appears to have been taken ill here with some dangerous disease. It was probably a return of the trouble which he had a few years before and which he called "a stake in his flesh." The reason why we think he was taken ill here is that he wrote afterwards to his friends in Galatia that he came to them because he had an illness, and he seems to have gone directly to Galatia now from Perga. The illness may quite likely have been malaria, though there is no way to prove it. The few references to his trouble have made some scholars think that it was malaria—a disease which comes back again and again and is dreadfully annoying to a person who wants to do a great work. The low land of Pamphilia may quite likely have brought on a new attack and compelled our travellers to move up to a higher and healthier region. Anyway whether this theory is correct or not, Paul and Barnabas decided to push on farther north to the hill country of Pisidia. This was the second of the three things. And the third was that Mark refused to go on with them. Something about the undertaking disturbed and frightened him. He turned back and went off home. Paul did not like Mark's desertion, but Barnabas, who was his uncle, did not treat it as quite so serious.

The two men now started off alone up over the hills and through the dangerous robber-infested country to the finely situated city of Antioch in Pisidia, which my reader must remember is very different from the other Antioch in Syria, from which Paul started on his journey. This second Antioch is in the Roman province of Galatia and we must now realise that on this first great missionary journey of his life Paul came to one of the cities of Galatia where, so far as we know, he founded the first of his missionary churches.

He began his work in the Jewish Synagogue in Antioch of Pisidia and he and Barnabas preached to the Jews of that city and to the other people who sympathised with them and who were called "God-fearers" because they were eager to learn about the God of the Jews. But after a little time the Jews disagreed with the message which the missionaries brought them and so Paul and Barnabas gave up trying to convince the Jews and set to work to tell their good news to the Greeks, just as they had done in Syrian Antioch, and these people flocked to hear them and believed their message with great joy, and were ready almost to pluck out their eyes and give them to Paul. From this first city of the Galatian province they went on to other important cities of the same province—Iconium, Derbe and Lystra. These four cities, we shall now assume, were the four centres of the churches of Galatia. One remarkable incident happened while

MAP OF THE COASTLINE
including the
NORTH-EAST CORNER of the MEDITERRANEAN,
showing the course of
ST PAUL'S SHIP
from the town of Myra

Paul and Barnabas were working in the city of Lystra. The simple country people here made up their minds that Paul and Barnabas must be gods come down from heaven to visit them and they brought out their oxen and were ready to sacrifice them to Barnabas and Paul, who they thought were Jupiter and Mercury. It was here in this very region around Lystra that Baucis and Philemon once lived. And according to the old Greek stories, Jupiter and Mercury came down to earth on a visit. They came looking like common men and nobody knew that they were gods and when they came to men's houses asking to be taken in and entertained, nobody would receive them. Finally they came to the poverty-stricken home of Baucis and Philemon, who received their visitors with much joy. They killed their only chicken for the supper and did the best they could to show true hospitality. Suddenly the two visitors stood forth as mighty gods. They blessed and thanked Baucis and Philemon and turned their humble dwelling into a splendid temple and glorified the two poor people who had received them so kindly.

Well, these simple people at Lystra evidently thought when they listened to Paul and Barnabas and saw their wonderful deeds that Jupiter and Mercury had come back again and they were resolved not to make a second mistake and miss the blessing. Paul and Barnabas had no desire to be treated as gods nor to have sacrifices made to them, but they had difficult work getting the simple hearted people to treat them as men and to drive their oxen home.

XIII

THE FIRST GREAT PROBLEM

PAUL and Barnabas had another experience at Lystra which was very different from that of being taken for gods. Paul's own people, the Jews, had begun to see now that he was not like them. He did not care for the things which were as important to them as life. His entire interest lay in telling not about Moses and his law but about Christ and the new life which men could live in His power. To the faithful Jews he seemed like a traitor. They did not want to hear him preach and they were determined to make him stop telling these new things to the people, if they possibly could.

The Jews got together from the cities which Paul and Barnabas had visited and they came in a body to Lystra and stirred up the fickle, changeable peasants and set them against the missionaries who had come to help them. They dragged them out of the city and stoned them until they thought they were dead. Paul must have thought of Stephen as the stones rained down upon him and he knew now how it felt to be stoned by the very people he wanted most to help. Fortunately the stones did not kill him. They only wounded him severely and when the mob had gone away he got up and came back into the city and preached again to his friends who had learned to love him and to believe in him. The next day he and Barnabas left Lystra and went to Derbe. Then they returned and revisited all the churches they had started in Galatia—in Derbe, Lystra, Iconium and Antioch of Pisidia, after which they went back to their home-church in great Antioch. It must have been a happy moment, as the two travellers sat in the midst of the group at

Antioch and told of the wonderful events of their long and dangerous journey and as they related how in the far-away province of Galatia they had built up new and flourishing churches out of people who just before had been ignorant heathen. But the happiness and joy were not long undisturbed, for some members of the church in Jerusalem came to Antioch and told the Christians there that Paul was wrong in his ideas and in his teaching, that Barnabas was wrong and that the church there in Antioch was wrong. These men insisted that nobody except Jews could be Christians. If any Gentile wanted to be a Christian and come into the church, they said that he must first be circumcised and become a Jew and he must keep the whole law of Moses. Christ came only for Jews, they said. If anybody went about teaching that Greeks and barbarians and men of all races and all customs could be Christ's followers, that man was wrong and was a dangerous teacher.

What these people said struck right against everything Paul was doing. According to their views most of the people in the church at Antioch were not real Christians. They would have to change all their ways of living. They would need to accept the whole system of Moses and all the sacrifices set forth in the Old Testament before they could have any part in Christ and His "good news."

Paul was determined not to yield to these men from Jerusalem and he saw that he must go to Jerusalem himself and prove to the whole church there that this idea that only Jews could be Christians was false. He must make them see that the new idea which he and the Christians at Antioch held was true and right; the idea that all men everywhere, of every race and of every colour and of every custom could follow Christ and come to God through Him and live by the power of His Spirit without becoming Jews at all.

Paul and Barnabas, with one of their new

converts, Titus, who was a Greek and who had
never become a Jew, went together to Jerusalem to have a council with the church there
and to settle forever, if they could, this important and difficult question.   Paul threw himself into the discussion with all the earnestness
and fire that were in his nature.   He brought
in Titus, as a specimen and exhibit of the kind
of Christians the Greeks made when they gave
their lives to Christ.   Paul refused to let
Titus be circumcised.   He declared that
Titus was already a full Christian without
doing anything to make himself a Jew.   As
Paul talked and showed what Christ meant to
him and told of the wonderful things Christ
had done through him the men in Jerusalem
who had been disciples of Christ were convinced that he was right and they gave him
their hands as a token of their faith in him and
of their regard for him.   But the other
members of the church were not yet ready for
the new teaching and the new ideas.   They

were old-fashioned people who could not change their habits. They listened to Paul and were impressed with his shining face and his glowing words, but when he was done speaking they thought just as they did before!

Soon after he had returned from the great conference in Jerusalem, when he thought he had convinced the church in Jerusalem that his position was the right one, he heard that men from Jerusalem had gone to the cities in Galatia and had told his new converts there —in Derbe and Lystra and Iconium and in Pisidia—that the two missionaries, who had recently visited them and had told them about Christ, were false teachers and had led them astray. These Jerusalem men worked upon the simple-minded Galatian people until they made them really believe that Paul and Barnabas were wrong. Their new visitors told the people in Galatia that they must go on now and become Jews. They must be circumcised and keep the law of Moses and they said that if they did that they could have the privilege of enjoying Christ.   But if they did not do *that*, then they could have no part in Christ.

It was an unspeakable shock to Paul when this piece of news reached him about his Galatian friends.   He saw how helpless they had been.   He realised how hard it would be to answer their visitors and he knew that these simple peasants were not to blame for being confused.   But he quickly saw that he must save them.   He must not let them go astray. He must come to their help and he must write them a letter that would open their eyes and show them the full truth.   I am inclined to think this letter was the first of all his wonderful epistles.   We must turn and see how the great leader wrote to his beloved friends and young disciples in the hill country of Galatia.

XIV

WHEN Paul sat down to write to the churches in the province of Galatia he was facing one of the greatest crises of his life. If he could not convince them that he was right in his teaching and that all men everywhere could follow Christ and become His disciples, then his missionary work was ended and his career was over. He had been proud once to be a Jew. He had gloried in the privilege of belonging to the chosen people and he had hoped to become perfectly righteous by keeping all the law and the commandments. He had tried this plan with all his energy and it had miserably failed. He had never made himself perfect and he had discovered that nobody ever could reach perfection that way.

Just at the moment when he realised his failure most, he had suddenly found Christ and through His life and power he had learned how to live in joy and peace and triumph. It was the most wonderful discovery! The whole world seemed new and all nature seemed changed! The whole business of his life was to go out and tell people everywhere about his discovery and what it meant.

And now these men from Jerusalem had gone out to his new churches and made them think that all his work was wrong, that all that he told them was false. They must become Jews. They must try with all their might to keep the law. They must do what Paul had endeavoured to do before he found Christ. They must strain and struggle on, all their lives, to make themselves good, and then, if they succeeded, they could enjoy Christ. It seemed to Paul a pitiful drop from his great and wonderful message. *He* could never go out and tell people that. If his dis-

covery and his message were not true, then he
could never go out again on a missionary
journey. There was nothing left for him but
to go back to Tarsus and make tents and then
to die and be buried like the rest of men.
Now if ever he must make his new converts
see and understand his discovery and he must
absolutely convince them that he was right
and that God was with him. That is what
the Epistle to the Galatians was written for.

Intense and eager and determined as he was,
he was also tender and loving. This letter is
all full of passages in which you can almost
feel this great man's heart throb. "You are,"
he tells them, "just like my own children. I
came to you when you were living in sin and
ignorance and, like a father full of love, I
helped you into a new life. I brought you to
Christ and I showed you how to get free from
your old bondage and how to rise into a life
of joy and power. I cannot bear to see you
drop back into bondage again. If you believe

what these visitors have told you, you will
never be free again, you will have to carry
burdens all your days." "When I came first
among you," he wrote, "you were full of joy.
You loved me and believed me, as though I
had been an angel or a god come to visit you.
You would have plucked out your eyes and
given them to me, if you could have done it.
I want now to be your friend and I want you
to believe that what I tell you is the truth."
Then he showed them how foolish was the
story which the Jews from Jerusalem had told
them. They had said that only those who
were "sons of Abraham" could share in the
promises of Christ. "Sons of Abraham,"
Paul cried out to them, "who are the real sons
of Abraham!" "Not those who become Jews
and keep the law but those who are full of
faith, who trust Christ and live by His power.
The most wonderful thing about Abraham
was his *faith*. He believed God. He trusted
God. He walked with God. He did not

keep the law, because the law was not given until many centuries after Abraham had died. If you want to be 'a son of Abraham' you must live by faith. You must trust God and take Christ for your leader, your helper, your inward strength."

He drew, in his letter, a wonderful picture of the true way to live. He gave his friends an account of his own life and told them they could also have what had come to him. "Why," he said, "God has revealed His Son in my soul. I used to do wrong and go wrong. I could not keep myself. I tried to live by the law but it would not work. Now I live by faith—faith in Christ, and the life I now live is really the life He lives in me. I do not care any more for the things people do to make themselves good. I feel Christ coming into me and giving me strength and power, just as the sun comes into the tree and builds its life from within. You can all have that power formed in you. You can all feel the

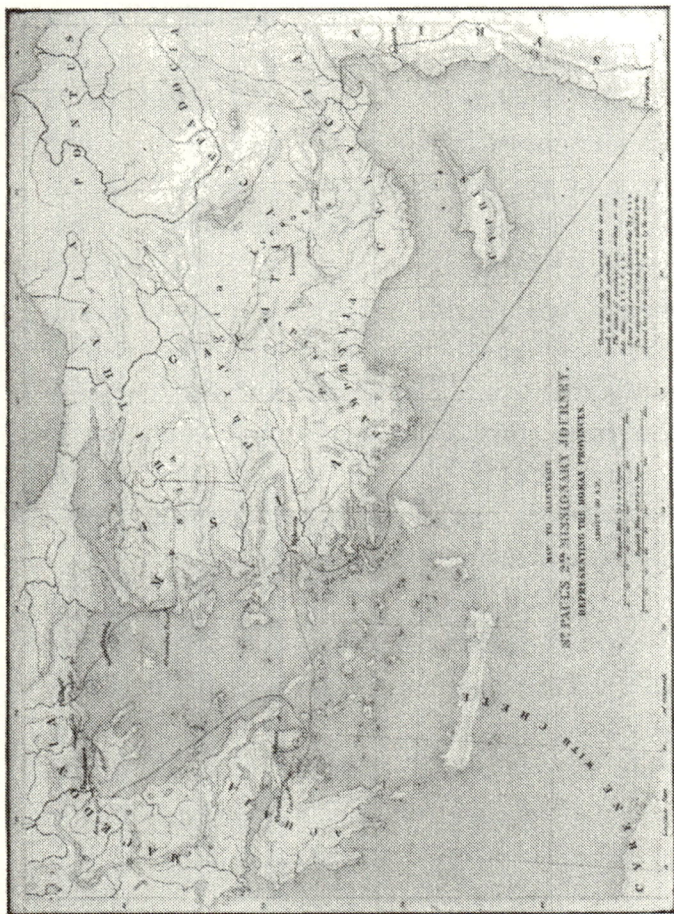

MAP TO ILLUSTRATE
ST. PAUL'S 2ND MISSIONARY JOURNEY,
REPRESENTING THE ROMAN PROVINCES
(ABOUT AD 51.)

force which will come into you and raise you out of your old self into a new way of life. Just that is what Christ does. When He helps you and comes into you, a new spirit is formed and you get love, joy, peace, patience, kindness, goodness, faithfulness, meekness, and endurance in your own souls. It is like discovering a new world. It is like a new creation. That is what Christ does. He makes people new creatures. These people who came to you from Jerusalem cannot tell you how to do that—but I can tell you. I bear in my body the marks of this new creation which Christ has formed in me."

Something like that Paul wrote to his friends in Galatia and the best of it is, they believed him and stood by him. When they had read his letter, they said: Paul is right. It is so. We will take his way. We will have Christ and not the law-system—and so Paul had won his first great battle.

XV

"COME OVER INTO MACEDONIA AND HELP US"

THE old heroes of Greece were heroes because they went out to fight with beasts and to free the world of terrible monsters. Then, again, there were heroes who fought with giants, or with deadly enemies of their country, and who risked their lives for their friends or for their people. Paul was a new kind of hero. His great battle was a battle with false ideas, a battle for the truth, a battle for the good news which Christ had brought to the world. It is harder to be this kind of a hero. Most people do not recognise the new kind of hero when he comes. They do not know that he *is* a hero. He often has to fight alone and he is misunderstood even by his

III

friends. Paul had many lonely hours. He could not have stood the strain and struggle if he had not been sure of Christ's presence and help and if he had not known that he was the champion of the greatest truth in the world.

Now that he had won the victory in this important contest in Galatia, and now that he had settled the question that Christ was the Saviour of all men of all races, he could go out again on another great out-reaching mission-ary journey. Paul wanted to go again with Barnabas, but Barnabas was determined to take Mark once more as companion and Paul was just as determined not to have Mark, be-cause he deserted them on their former jour-ney, so that they finally agreed to separate. Barnabas went to Cyprus with Mark, and Paul took a companion named Silas, and started out without quite knowing what coun-try he would travel to before his return. He and Silas went, probably by land, through the

Syrian gate in the mountains, to Tarsus and visited the Christian settlements in the province of Cilicia, then directly on to see his friends in Galatia who had been through so much since he saw them last. How we wish we knew what he said to them and what they said to him! But we do not know a single word that passed while Paul was living among the disciples of Galatia. We only know that he decided to take one of these Galatian Christians along with him as a helper in his work. This was a young man named Timothy whose home was in Derbe. He became one of Paul's greatest friends and a wonderful help to him, clear through to the end of his life. Being with Paul made Timothy a hero too.

After the three men had visited all the communities of Galatia, they started off toward the north and visited the cities in the district of Phrygia which belonged to the province of Galatia, and then they decided to strike across west and visit the great cities of the province of Asia, the capital of which was Ephesus, but they soon felt that the time had not come yet for this journey. They next tried to go to the country lying along the shores of the Black Sea, but something made them realise that this was not the right course for them to take, so that they went on to Troas on the shores of the Ægean Sea, without quite knowing where they would go next. Troas was the site of the old city of Troy where the Greeks and Trojans fought for ten years, and where some of the bravest deeds were done that the world ever saw. Here was the tomb of Achilles. Here Alexander the Great had come on his way to the conquest of the world. A greater conqueror had now come to Troas. Alexander went toward the east for his victories; the new conqueror was to go west!

While they were here in Troas without any clear plan of action, Paul felt in his soul that the next course was to sail across the Ægean

Sea into Europe. He felt it so clearly and
strongly that it seemed to him as though he
heard a man from the European side of the
sea calling to him and saying: "Come across
into Macedonia and bring us help." But it
was more than Macedonia that was calling.
It was the whole of Greece. It was more
than Greece that was calling. It was the
whole of Europe. It was more than Europe
that was calling. It was undiscovered
America that was stretching out its hands that
night and saying: "Come over and help us."
You see, if Paul had not gone into Europe,
across the Ægean, perhaps we who live in
America and in England would never have
been followers of Christ, so that this call meant
very much! Paul heard it and he was
"ready" at once. He answered: "Yes, I
will come." The next morning he set sail
from Troas on the eastern shore to Philippi on
the western shore of the Ægean. Silas and
Timothy were with him and he also found

here a new companion. This new travelling-
companion kept a Diary and wrote the account of this journey and of other journeys,
too. You can find his Diary in the sections
of the Book of Acts that say "we"—"the We
Narratives." Philippi in Macedonia is the
first spot in Europe on which Paul set his foot
and so far as we know the people in Philippi
were the first people of all Europe who heard
of Christ. They were not as eager to hear as
you might expect. If they were calling to
Paul to come over and help them, they did not
recognise him when he arrived, for they very
soon seized him and put him in prison and
beat him with rods. Some of the people
in Philippi, however, did recognise him.
They were very glad to hear him and they
were full of love for him and for his truth.
They joined him and worked with him and a
new church was formed—perhaps the first in
all Europe. These Christians in Philippi
were very dear to Paul's heart and they loved

him as though he had been their own father,
and they remembered him later when he lay
in prison in Rome and was lonely. When he
left Philippi, he went on through the great
cities of Macedonia, preaching and building
up churches, wherever he could find people
ready to listen to his message. In the city of
Thessalonica, which is now called Salonika,
Paul found many listeners and formed a successful church to which a little later he wrote
two epistles. He found another splendid
group in the city of Berœa and formed a
church there. But in all these cities of Macedonia he had serious trouble, just as he had
had in the province of Galatia. The Jews
hated him and everywhere he came they
raised a riot and tried to drive him out of the
city or to get him into prison. They set the
mob against him in some of the cities and in
others they had him arrested and badly
treated. But in spite of all their efforts to
hinder him, he succeeded in doing a great

work and in forming Christian churches all up and down the famous province of Macedonia.

From the time Paul heard the voice calling him over into Macedonia, most of the rest of his life was to be lived and most of his future work in the world was to be done around the shores of the Ægean Sea. All the churches which he gathered after this time were around the Ægean and all his epistles from this time were written either to Ægean cities, or written while he was living in Ægean cities. It was Paul who shifted the centre of Christianity from Jerusalem to the Western World and during his life-time the great centres were around the shores of this famous Sea. The most famous of all the cities around the coasts of this Sea was Athens, the home of Socrates and Plato and of a hundred other great men, and to this wonderful city of the ancient world Paul now came.

XVI

ALONE IN ATHENS

As Paul's two companions, Silas and Timothy, had been left behind in Berœa to finish the work which had been begun in Macedonia Paul found himself "alone in Athens." It was the most interesting city in the world for a traveller to visit. It was the "eye of Greece" and Greece had for five hundred years been leading the world in art, in poetry, in philosophy, in architecture and in many other things. The most beautiful temples that had ever been built were there for Paul to see. The most wonderful statues that had ever been carved were there for him to gaze upon. The most perfect poems that had ever been written were in the libraries there in Athens for him to read. A short walk would

take him to the garden of the Academe where
Plato once had his school.   He could stand
where Socrates stood.   He could see the home
of Stoic philosophy which he had heard about
all his life.   He was under the most perfect
sky the sun shines through.   He looked over
the glorious hills where great deeds had been
wrought.   Delightful air wrapped him round
and inspiring sights met him at every turn.

But Paul thought little of these things.
His mind was filled with something else which
seemed to him more important.   He wanted
to make this famous city see what he saw.   He
wanted to build a church of Christ in the city
that had built the Parthenon.   He wanted to
tell his message of truth to the people who
gloried in the wisdom of Plato and Aristotle.
As he was walking about alone in the city, he
noticed an altar with the inscription on it:
"To God Unknown."   At once, he thought,
"How I should like to make these people know
the God whom I know, but whom they have

not found yet. They want to find Him, or
they would not build altars like that. All
their philosophers have wanted to find Him,
and sometimes they almost did find Him.
Oh, if I could only make them see!" While
Paul was walking around the city, wishing
for a chance to tell his message, the Athenian
people in the streets and market-places were
watching him. They saw at once that he was
a stranger and of a different race. They noticed him gazing around. Some of them
asked him questions and sounded him to see
whether he brought any new ideas. But they
did not expect much from a mere Jew. They
thought from the little they listened to that
he believed in two gods—or a god and a goddess—whom they had never heard of before,
for he spoke of Jesus and of the resurrection.
They thought Jesus was a new god and that
the Resurrection was a new goddess. But
most of the people thought that he was a
"babbler"—a man who was talking about

trifles.   They never dreamed that this foreign
visitor, this Jew, could teach them, wise
Athenians as they were, anything that mat-
tered to them.   But some of the inquisitive
and curious ones got Paul to come up to their
great meeting-place on the Hill of Mars,
which they called the Areopagus, and speak
to them.   That was exactly what Paul
wanted.   Now he had a chance to tell them
his great truth.   Would they listen?   Would
they understand?

With a polite wave of the hand, he began
to speak in the Greek which he had learned
as a boy at Tarsus.   "Athenian men," he said,
"you are very religious people.   I see altars
everywhere and you have filled your city with
objects of worship.   One strange thing I noticed as I walked about.   I saw an altar on
which was this inscription, 'To God Unknown.'   That means that you have not quite
found God yet.   Let me tell you about Him,
for I know.   He made the world.   He made

MARS HILL — ATHENS

all things above and all things beneath. But
He does not dwell in temples. He does not
need the things which men make with their
hands, idols and images and statues. He has
given life and breath to all living beings. He
has planned the universe and put His wisdom
into all the parts of it. He has arranged
everything for men. He expects them to become one great family. He has put something into men's hearts which makes them seek
after Him and which makes them try to feel
their way, as blind persons do, to find Him if
they can. But He is never far away from
anybody. He is near, within reach. We
live in God. We move in Him. All our life
is flooded with Him, and without Him we
could not live at all. Your poets knew that.
They have tried to tell you about it. One of
them in his poem says that we are 'offspring of
God'—we have come from Him. If that is
true, as your poet says it is, you ought not to
think that God is like silver or gold or marble,

or that He can be carved and made into a statue. All that is childlike and is the result of ignorance. When men were in the child stage and did not know any better, God excused them and waited for them to learn. But now that you are older and wiser, there is no excuse. God expects everybody now to live differently, to change their lives, and to prepare for the great beyond. He has sent His Son to show them how to do it, and He has raised Him from the dead."

They did not listen very well and when they found that the Resurrection was not a new goddess they were not interested any longer. They drifted away to look for something that was more exciting and they politely told Paul that they would hear him again some other time. One man who was a senator and one woman, who had listened eagerly, were convinced that this was the truth about God and they believed and accepted Paul's way of life. But Athens was not ready yet for the great message and so the chance went by! In a few days Paul sailed away, out of that wonderful harbour, looking back on the beautiful city that had missed its opportunity, and landed in the great seaport city of Corinth, at that time the capital of the province of Achaia.

XVII

CORINTH AND EPHESUS

I,N Corinth Paul made two new friends
who became very dear to him and who were
able to be great helpers in his work. Their
names were Aquila—a Jew from Pontus who
had lived sometime in Italy—and his wife
Priscilla who was a very remarkable woman.
They became followers of Christ and joined
with Paul in the work of spreading Christianity in the great Greek city of Corinth.
Aquila and Priscilla were also tent-makers
and part of the time they all worked at this
trade to get money to live by. Then they gave
all the rest of their time to the main business
for which Paul had come to Corinth. It was
a very happy group of workers for they all
loved and enjoyed each other and they all

loved and enjoyed their work. As Corinth
was a great city close to the sea, people from
all countries in the world came there.   There
were men of many colours and men of many
languages.   They had not learned how to live
good and beautiful lives.   Very wrong things
were done in Corinth.   We sometimes think
that the world is wicked to-day but if we could
see the way the Corinthians lived and then see
how men live to-day we should discover that
there has been some improvement.

For a year and a half, this little group of
missionaries laboured in the city, telling about
Christ and His love and His death for men
and His resurrection and of His Spirit working in the hearts of men.   All kinds of people were changed by the power of this message. Jews and Greeks and persons from
many lands listened and rejoiced and believed
and followed Christ.   Paul's old enemies, the
Jews, who had heard about his past life, made
all the trouble they could for him, but he had

been through trouble before and he knew how to bear it now. He went straight ahead with his work and was not disturbed by the difficulties. His soul was filled with joy as he saw his little church growing larger every day. New persons kept coming and there were more all the time who were trying to live the new way. All kinds of people came in to form the new church in Corinth. A few of them were learned and well off, but most of them were poor and ignorant. They were working people who had never had any real *life* before, and now the whole world seemed changed for them. It was as though they had been living in a dark cave before and now they had come into the beautiful world where the bright sun was shining.

After eighteen months of this hard and happy work, Paul, with his two companions, and with his two new friends, sailed away from Corinth, leaving behind a great group of Christian men and women and children

EPHESUS

gathered into a church.   We can well believe
that all these people, who had found the new
life, were on the shore of the harbour at
Cenchrea to say "farewell" and to wave their
last greetings as the missionaries pushed out
to sea.   They sailed in and out among the
famous islands of the Ægean and across its
blue waters to the eastern shore and came to
Ephesus.   Paul had wanted to go to Ephesus
at the beginning of this long missionary journey, but he had not been able to accomplish
his desire then.   Now after wonderful expe-
riences, dangers and trials and after many
months of work in Europe he found himself at
last in the great city of Ephesus.   He knew
that this was to be one of the most important
fields of his entire lifework, but he still felt
that the time for his work in Ephesus had not
come yet.   So he left Aquila and Priscilla
there and went on by ship to Cæsarea and then
to his beloved home church group at Antioch.

There were many things to tell as the Christian Jews and Greeks of Antioch flocked in to hear Paul recount the wonderful events of the greatest journey of his life. How the field had widened and how Christianity had spread in these eventful years since he last saw Antioch! After a short stay at Antioch, Paul went once more, and this was to be the last time, to see his dear friends in Galatia. When this visit was finished, he came over the great stretch of country which formed the ancient province of Asia to its capital, Ephesus. He had made a little beginning of work here before his return to Antioch and now he came back to finish what he had begun.

Ephesus was much larger than Corinth and it was also, like Corinth, a very wicked city. There was much to do here and much to suffer before Ephesus could be changed into a city of pure and beautiful citizens. But nothing ever discouraged Paul. He went at his great task as though he fully expected to see it done. It was like fighting beasts in the arena to work among the hard and wicked people who tried every way they could to defeat Paul and spoil his work. Steadily he fought on—gaining a little all the time—explaining to everybody who came to hear and proving that he had found a new way to live.

Right in the midst of this great work of transforming and remaking Ephesus, Paul heard very bad news from Corinth, across the Ægean. He heard that the church there was in sad trouble. The people had divided into parties and were quarrelling. Some of the people had gone wrong and were doing the kind of things they used to do when they were heathen. Paul wrote a wonderful letter to them—our First Corinthians. It was full of good advice and counsel and it showed them how to get back into the new way of living. The most wonderful thing in the letter was what Paul said to them about love. He told them, in the most beautiful words that perhaps were ever written that love was the

greatest thing in the world, that when everything else failed love would not fail and when
everything else vanished away love would still
abide.

You would have thought this letter would
have settled all their troubles but it did not.
When people get wrong it is very hard setting
them right again and it often takes a long time
and much patience.   Things went from bad
to worse.   Finally Paul had to leave his work
in Ephesus and go across to Corinth, to see the
people there in person and to straighten out
their trouble.   But even when he got among
them, they remained stubborn and difficult,
and he had to go back without getting the
trouble settled.   Then he sent Timothy over
and he failed.   It looked as though the
church would fall to pieces and Paul would
lose all his friends in Corinth.   Then he
wrote another letter, full of pleading, which
he sent by his friend Titus, who was now his
companion.

While he was waiting, full of anxiety, for Titus to come back with the answer from Corinth, some dreadful catastrophe happened in Ephesus. There was a great uprising in the city against Paul. It seemed for a time as though there was no hope that his life could be saved. He has told us that the sentence of death was pronounced against him—probably the sentence that he should be thrown into the arena to fight with lions. For a time there seemed no hope. But his friends Aquila and Priscilla, whom Paul sometimes calls "Prisca," saved his life. He says that they "risked their necks" for him and that he was "delivered from death."

This catastrophe may very likely be connected in some way with the strange event so powerfully described in the nineteenth chapter of Acts. It happened this way. There was a man in Ephesus named Demetrius. He was a silversmith and made little silver images of the goddess Diana which he sold in great numbers to the people. These images were little copies of the great statue of Diana which the Ephesians believed had fallen down from heaven, and so it was looked upon with awe and was very sacred. One of the most beautiful temples in the world—one of the seven "wonders"—had been built to Diana in Ephesus and in this temple stood the famous statue. Now Demetrius made a great deal of money selling his silver images to those who visited the temple. But suddenly he discovered that people were not buying as many of his silver Dianas as they used to do. He began to wonder what was happening and he hit upon the idea that all the trouble was caused by the preaching of Paul! Paul was calling people to Christ and when they believed in Christ, they no longer worshipped Diana. They stopped going to her temple and they did not care to have copies of the great statue. Demetrius was losing money. His business was in danger.   Something must

be done. He called together all the silver-
smiths and stirred them up to do something
at once to drive Paul out of the city. "Just
see," he cried, "how our trade is going down!
We are losing all our business! We are making no money! This stranger has come to
our city and he has told people that gods are
not made of silver and gold; that gods made
by hands are no gods at all! He has carried
people away with his new ideas. They won't
buy our images now. Not only is our business in danger, but our whole city will suffer
as well. People will stop coming to see the
great temple which all the world admired.
We must act. We must save the city and
defend the great goddess!" Then all the
silversmiths and goldsmiths and coppersmiths
and workers in iron and brass began to make
processions through the city, shouting as they
marched, "Great is Diana of the Ephesians."
"Great is Diana of the Ephesians." The
whole city was aroused. People rushed out

of their houses to see what was happening
and a great commotion and excitement followed.   The throng pressed into the immense
city theatre and everybody kept shouting,
some one thing and some another, as generally happens in a vast mob of excited people.
Paul tried to get into the theatre.   He was,
as usual, ready to face the danger and stand
his ground.   But his friends kept him back
and would not let him risk his life in such a
wild and seething and furious crowd.   When
any one tried to speak the mob drowned the
voice of the speaker with their shouts.   A
man named Alexander—perhaps he was
"Alexander, the coppersmith," who, Paul
says, did him "much evil," a little later—tried
to speak, when suddenly the vast throng of
excited people began crying again, "Great is
Diana of the Ephesians."   " Great is Diana
of the Ephesians."   For two hours nobody
could stop this cry which went on and on,
with the continual shout, "Great is Diana of

TEMPLE OF DIANA

the Ephesians." At last the town-clerk of the city got the people quiet and made a sensible speech to them, telling them if they had any charge against Paul the right thing to do was to take the matter to the courts and not to get up a riot and endanger the liberty and reputation of the city. Then he sent the people away to their homes.

How this uproar affected Paul we do not know. What danger threatened him now because of the hate of Demetrius and the silver-smiths we cannot tell. Nobody knows exactly what happened, but in some way Paul escaped from the city, never to go back again. He got to Troas in safety and then crossed over the Ægean at the same place where he crossed the first time he entered Europe, and reached Macedonia where he was among his friends.

Here in Macedonia where Paul was waiting, worn and perplexed and weary—but not cast down—Titus came to him from Corinth and told him the good news that his letter to Corinth had done its work, had saved the day, and that now his church there was ready to be faithful to him.   Nothing in his life ever touched his soul with more joy than did that report which Titus brought.   If you wish to see how he felt, you must read the first nine chapters of Second Corinthians, for he wrote those chapters just after Titus came to him. It makes you love Paul to find how eagerly he loved his friends and his churches, and to see how much he suffered when they did wrong or turned against him.   Soon after this he went to Corinth and spent three months there with his old and new friends of that city.

XVIII

" READY TO BE BOUND "

THERE were many things to do in Corinth, on this last visit of Paul's life to the city where he had worked so long and suffered so much. He had many things to tell them. There were many changes to make in the management of the church. There were many families to visit and all the time there were new people being added to the church. Then Paul was raising a great fund of money which he hoped to carry up to Jerusalem on his return, for the support of the church in that city. Finally he had letters to write to his other churches, advice to give them, difficulties to settle and problems to solve. Perhaps the most important thing he did during this stay in Corinth—certainly the most important for us—was to write a letter, which we now call an Epistle, to the Christians in the city of Rome. It is the longest of all Paul's Epistles and the one in which he sets forth most carefully and fully his entire message about Christ. He had not been to Rome yet and he had not met the Christians there, but he was planning to go to Rome, after he had been to Jerusalem, on his way to Spain and he wanted to prepare the Christians in the great capital of the empire for the teaching which he expected to give them when he arrived. He little thought as he was writing this wonderful letter that when he did come to Rome he would come chained to two soldiers and that this would be the end of his journey! He told the people at Rome, in this letter, how hard he had tried as a young man to make himself perfect, how he had resolved to keep the law and be absolutely righteous, and how miserably he had failed. "When I meant to do right," he wrote, "I did wrong."

"The things I wanted to do I did not do. The
things I did, were just those things which I
ought not to have done. And when I was
defeated and beaten and hopeless then suddenly I discovered the love of God which
Christ revealed to me. I found a power to
live by, which delivered me from the old
power of sin in my nature. Now through
that love and that power I am more than
conqueror. I know now that nothing can
ever separate me from the love of God.
Neither death nor life, nor angels, nor prin-
cipalities, nor powers, nor things present, nor
things to come, nor height, nor depth, nor anything that has ever been made in the universe,
can separate me from the love of God in
Christ Jesus."

He told these unseen friends of his in the
far-away city how to live the new way day by
day in the difficult world. He told them not
to overcome evil by doing evil in return but to
overcome it by being good and by doing good.

He told them not to worry, or fret, or be disturbed, when things were hard and difficult, but to keep calm and steady and full of faith in the love of God, and when they had done the best they could, to leave it all with God. They were, as far as possible, to live in peace and love with all kinds of people and no matter what others did to them, they were to go right on loving them and doing good to them.

When he had sent off his great epistle, and had done all that he could to strengthen the church in Corinth and had received a large collection for Jerusalem and had gathered his friends around him, Paul said farewell to Corinth and started on his return journey, accompanied by a number of companions. He went back through Macedonia—Berœa, Thessalonica, Philippi—and then across the Ægean to Troas where he had first heard the call to go to Europe. There must have been a church there on "the plains of windy Troy," for Paul remained seven days and held meet-

ings far into the night, but we do not know
very much about this church by the Simois
River—only that one of the young men there
went to sleep while the meeting was going on
and fell out of a window in the third story to
the ground! Here at Troas Paul found again
his old friend, the writer of the Diary—"the
We Narrative"—who joined the party for the
journey to Jerusalem. They went part of the
way by land and part of the way by sea, stop-
ping at Assos and Mitylene, touching at the
famous island of Samos, and disembarking at
Miletus. Here at Miletus, the leaders of the
church at Ephesus came down to see the man
whom they had learned to love, to hear his
message and to say farewell to him. It was
probably not safe for Paul to go to Ephesus
with its beasts. There were too many dangers
there for him. After all his years of work and
his perils in that city it was a joy to see the
men and women with whom he had lived and
laboured and to have one more chance to

speak to them about the highest things in life.
It was a very solemn time as they gathered on
the seashore and Paul told them of the
troubles and dangers that lay before them
and before him. He then told them that they
would never see each other again. They
loved him as though he had been a father to
each one and they all wept as he left them to
go into the ship to sail for Syria. As they
went on their way Paul realised, from what
he heard at every port where the ship stopped,
that it would be very dangerous for him in
Jerusalem. He had not been in the Holy City
since the great conference there with Peter
and James and John. Since that time tremendous things had happened across the world.
Paul had succeeded, but the more he succeeded the more the Jews hated him. They
had made trouble for him in every city.
They had come to regard him as a traitor and
as the enemy of their race and they were
eager to get rid of him forever. He knew

how they felt. He saw the danger ahead.
He understood that if he went to Jerusalem it
would be like going into the lion's mouth.
But he was determined to go, danger or no
danger, for Paul was a hero. He had a great
gift to carry up to the poor and needy Christians in Jerusalem and he must have thought
that he could win them over and make them
see his truth at last. He believed that this
was the greatest opportunity of his life. Perhaps now, after all the wonderful work
around the Ægean Sea he might be able to
make his own people see the truth that had
meant so much to the Greeks and to the Galatians. Perhaps now he could join both
branches together—those who were Jewish
Christians and those who were Gentile-Chris-
tians—and have one great world church with
no division in it. It was worth trying any-
how. It was worth any kind of risk. The
great gift would soften their hearts and he
would plead with them, and then it would be

done! When prophets on the way told Paul how dangerous the risk was, he said to them: "Do not talk to me of danger. Do not try to change my course. I am *ready,* not only to be bound in Jerusalem, but if necessary to die there for this cause"—and on he went, like the hero he was.

He very soon found that he was in the midst of enemies. James told him that there were many thousands of Christian-Jews who had heard serious charges against him, how he no longer kept the law of Moses and how he taught his converts that they did not need to become Jews, or to do the things which all good Jews considered necessary and he showed Paul how stern they were sure to be toward him.

He had hardly begun to live in Jerusalem when some Jews discovered him in the city. They gave a cry and raised a mob and rushed at him and seized him. They were so furious that they nearly killed him on the spot, but a Roman captain with a troop of soldiers came up just in time to rescue him and to carry him away to the military castle where the mob could not get at him. But he could hear them cry and shout: "Away with him! away with him!"

XIX

IN THE PRISON AT CÆSAREA

STANDING on the steps of the castle, with the angry, surging people in front of him Paul beckoned for silence and then spoke to the most difficult audience he ever addressed. He calmly told them the story of his life. He gave them an account of that great moment on the road to Damascus when Jesus met him and called him to a new life and a new mission. He explained to them how he tried to tell the good news to his own people and how God sent him to the great world of Gentiles. Then, all of a sudden, the people cried out in a fury: "Away with such a fellow from the earth." They threw off their garments and would have ended his life in a moment if they could have reached him. It was another scene like the one which occurred when Jesus was on his way to Calvary, and when Stephen was being hurried out of the gates of Jerusalem and Paul himself held the garments of the men who threw the stones.

This time the crowd was powerless for they could not get their victim. The soldiers guarded him and took him into the castle where he was to be scourged, that is beaten with rods. The soldiers tied Paul up to the wall with thongs and were ready to begin the terrible scourging when he quietly asked the centurion if it was lawful to scourge a Roman citizen who had not been found guilty of any crime. The centurion went out and told the chief captain that Paul was a Roman, and he immediately stopped the scourging. The next day Paul had an opportunity to address the great council of the Jews in the presence of Ananias, the high-priest, but the council divided in their opinion of Paul, some approving of him and some disapproving, until they

nearly tore him in pieces in their excitement.
Once more the soldiers saved him by rushing in and carrying him away to the castle.
Meantime, a band of men got together and
formed a secret plot to kill Paul and have
done with him. This time it was not the
Roman soldiers who saved him. It was his
nephew. Paul, we remember, had a sister in
Jerusalem. And in some way her son discovered this plot. He got into the castle and
told his uncle, who brought him to a centurion and the centurion took the young man
to the chief captain where he told all he knew
of the plot. The brave boy saved his uncle's
life, for the chief captain, when he heard the
boy's story, ordered two hundred soldiers and
seventy horsemen and two hundred spearmen
to take Paul by night to Cæsarea, where the
Roman governor had his home and head-
quarters and where Paul would be safe until
his trial was over. He was taken at first to
Herod's palace, though we may be pretty sure

that the part in which Paul lived was more
like a prison than a palace, but this wonderful
man had something in his soul which changed
even prisons into palaces.

Soon after his arrival, Ananias, the high-
priest, with a lawyer named Tertullus, came
down to Cæsarea to lay before Felix, the
Roman governor, the charges against Paul.
Tertullus made a speech charging Paul with
being "a pestilent fellow," "a mover of insur-
rections" up and down the empire wherever
he travelled. He said Paul was "a ringleader
of the Nazarenes" and that he did things con-
trary to the laws and customs of the Jews.
Tertullus made out as bad a case as he could
and the other Jews who had come down with
him added whatever they could think of
against the prisoner.

Then Felix made a sign that Paul might
speak in his own defence. He declared, in
calm and persuasive words that he had never
wilfully stirred up the crowd, or encouraged a

riot. He told the governor that his whole business in the world was to live the way of life that God had revealed as the true way. A little later Paul spoke again before Drusilla, a Jewess, who was Felix's wife. He spoke so powerfully this time of righteousness and self-control and the perfect way of life and of the future of joy and woe, that the old Roman governor trembled as he listened. But he did not change his life. He was weak of will and he had woven a chain of habits which he could not break. He had heard that Paul had brought great sums of money to Jerusalem and he hoped that Paul would offer a large bribe for his liberty so that Felix kept him in prison two years. Felix saw him occasionally and gave him a chance to offer a bribe, which never was offered! Thus two long years dragged by. Paul was longing to go on with the work that had been changing the world. He was eager to see his old friends and to help them in their troubles, but all the time he was fast bound with chains in the strong prison at Cæsarea. There is in the Second Epistle to Timothy a fragment of a letter which Paul may have written from Cæsarea. He asks Timothy to bring him the cloak which he left at Troas. The prison by the sea was a cold place. And more touching still, he asks him to bring his books—I wish we knew the titles of these books—and his pieces of parchment, so that he could write letters to his churches and to his friends. After two years had dragged by, there came a change of governors. Porcius Festus succeeded Felix. The Jerusalem Jews made a great effort to prejudice the new governor against Paul and he proposed to push the trial through at once and have the case settled. It was evident that Paul could hardly have a fair trial in Cæsarea. The Jews were full of passion against him. They were ready to use all the ways known to them to secure his condemnation and death. And Paul saw that he had little chance of escape in the local court, so that as the crisis approached he used his privilege as a Roman citizen and appealed to be tried before Cæsar in Rome, and Festus immediately granted the appeal.

Before the time came for Paul to start on his momentous journey to Rome, King Agrippa and his wife Bernice came to Cæsarea to bring greetings to the new governor and they heard from Festus of the famous prisoner who had appealed to Cæsar. King Agrippa very much desired to see Paul and to hear him speak and Festus arranged for Agrippa to hear him. The king sat on a throne with much splendour. All the distinguished persons of the court were there. Soldiers with helmets and with the Roman eagles were stationed round the hall. And into the midst Paul was led by his guard and then was given permission to speak. It was a great moment for the prisoner. His one thought was to make some of these people understand his great message. Once more he told the story of his life and how the light had shined upon him at Damascus and how he had obeyed the heavenly message which came to him then. He thought he might make the king Agrippa see that God always meant to send His Son to bring light and life to the world and he was telling him about the great prophecies in the Old Testament when suddenly Festus interrupted. He told Paul that he was wild and deluded, that he had thought over these things until he had lost his reason. Unmoved Paul answered and said "I am not deluded. I am calm and sober. I am talking about things which are absolutely certain and real. King Agrippa knows that these things are so." Then turning to the king, he said, "King Agrippa dost thou believe what our prophets have said? I know that thou must believe."

Then king Agrippa found it difficult to answer. It would not do to have a prisoner go

on talking that way to a king and yet this prisoner seemed to be right. King Agrippa
shrugged his shoulders and said: "With a
very little argument you seem to think you can
make *me* a Christian!" Paul with dignity
raised his chained hands and said: "Whether
my argument is little or great, I would to
God that not only thou but everybody here
who hears me speak to-day might feel what I
feel, and see what I see, and have the kind of
life I have and become such a person as I am
—only without these chains which are on my
hands!"

After Paul had retired King Agrippa said
to Festus: "If this man had not appealed to
Cæsar he might have been set free."

XX

THE STORMY JOURNEY TO ROME

THE journey from Cæsarea to Rome was at best a long and dangerous one. Paul was accustomed to the sea, for he had taken sea voyages ever since his early youth. He had already been shipwrecked three times and once he had clung to a piece of the wreck for twenty-four hours before he was rescued. But this was the first time he had gone on board ship as a prisoner and it was a new experience to be at sea in the charge of soldiers. The change from the prison in Cæsarea to the ship was, however, a welcome one, and now at last he was going to Rome and, he hoped, to freedom.

He was in the charge of the Augustan cohort, with Julius for centurion and there were other prisoners besides himself. A little band of friends attended him and among them was the writer of the famous "We-Diary" who has given us a wonderful account of this journey. The ship touched first at Sidon where the good-hearted centurion allowed Paul to go on shore, to visit his friends and to have a good home meal, which must have been a welcome change after the long tedious period of prison fare. Then they sailed under the lee of Cyprus and skirted the shore of Paul's beloved Cilicia. There were the mountains of his childhood in the distance—Amanus in the east, Taurus in the west. He could see the gleaming of the Cydnus on its way to the sea and imagination pictured the beautiful city on both banks of the river where he played and dreamed as a boy—the city he would never see again. Next came Pamphylia on whose shores he had landed years before and his mind ran on over the hills to a precious group of churches in the cities of Galatia.

From the city of Myra in the province of

Lycia they found an Alexandrian ship sailing for Italy and the centurion transferred his prisoners to it. They went far to the south of the Ægean, around whose shores the great work of Paul's life had been done and where now groups of friends were praying for him. The ship took them to the south of the great island of Crete and finally the wind forced them to put into Fair Havens near the middle of the island. Paul warned the centurion not to go on because of the certain danger of the voyage in the stormy season, but the master of the vessel was determined to have the ship sail and as soon as a favourable wind appeared they launched forth. But the ship had not been long at sea when a Mediterranean hurricane struck it and drove it on through the desperate waters. The ship was wrenched and twisted by the fury of the storm and it leaked seriously so that the sailors were compelled to put undergirding around it to tighten up the seams. In the fearful danger

they threw overboard the freight which the
ship was carrying and finally they threw out
the tackling and furniture of the ship to make
it as light as possible.   For fourteen days and
nights they floundered about in the Sea of
Adria at the mercy of the wind and the
boisterous billows.   No sun appeared by day
and the nights were appallingly dark.   Fear
lay on everybody except one and all hope was
gone in the minds of everybody but one.   This
one man had no fear and he was full of hope
and confidence.   He had never seen battles
such as the centurion with his cohort had been
through, but he had passed through great ex-
periences and he had learned to trust God
absolutely.   He had received five terrible
beatings from the Jews; three times he had
been given the Roman scourge.   He had been
in many prisons.   He had faced death again
and again on his journeys.   He had often
been where no escape seemed possible, when
an unexpected door had opened and he had

gone on in safety. He was the man, then, for this dreadful hour. He had the hero spirit and he could calm the others and kindle their courage.

Suddenly he stepped forth on deck and spoke to the men: "Be full of cheer and hope . We shall come through. My God has told me so. And I believe God. His I am. Him I serve and I know that He has given me all who sail with me in the ship. Not a life shall be lost!"

Then when the sailors had sounded and had found the water growing shallow they threw out four anchors and waited for morning to come. We have just seen that Paul had four anchors, too—four anchors to his soul: "I believe God"; "His I am"; "Him I serve"; "He has given me those who sail with me." In the morning they loosened the four anchors and let the sea drive the ship toward the shore at a place where two seas met and formed a cove, and there they beached it.

The force of the waves broke the ship to pieces
and the soldiers were for killing all the prisoners but the centurion had learned to respect
Paul and was determined to save him, so that
he allowed everybody on board to swim or
float to shore and all were saved. The island
turned out to be Malta, south of Sicily. Here
the ship's crew and the soldiers and the prisoners spent three months. Paul was able here
once again to preach to the people and he
worked wonders among them. At the end of
the three months they started out again on the
treacherous sea to complete the journey. The
ship on which they sailed from Malta bore
the sign of "the Twins," Castor and Pollux,
who were supposed by the Romans to be the
guardians of sailors. The new ship touched
at Syracuse, the famous capital of Sicily,
where Plato had come with his wisdom, and,
after two days, it brought its precious load
into port at Puteoli, near Naples, in sight of a
beautiful, quiet mountain peak, named Vesu-

vius, which, a few years later, was to spout
lava and cinders over the towns lying on the
shores of this wonderful blue bay. Here in
the Italian port, Paul found a group of Christian believers who greatly refreshed him, and
his kind centurion allowed him to stay there
an entire week. These Christians at Puteoli
were the first people in Italy to hear the great
teacher of the new way of life. Then on foot
or by horses, the strange troop wound up the
glorious valley, leading from Puteoli to
Rome. At the Forum of Appius, about ten
miles out of the imperial city, a band of
Roman Christians came to meet him as though
he were a hero coming in triumph to their
city. They found a prisoner kept by soldiers. When Paul saw these devoted Christian men coming to share their love and fellowship with him he forgot all about being
a prisoner. Here were dear friends who
loved him and that was enough. The long
and arduous journey of many months was

over.   Here in front was Rome.   Nero might
be there, and his court and prison might be
waiting for him, but the most important thing
was that there was a church of Christ in Rome
and Paul could see the members and make the
church grow larger!

XXI

THE TRIUMPH OF THE HERO

"I AM not ashamed of the gospel of Christ," Paul had said in his letter to Rome. "It is the *power* of God." Rome was the most powerful city the world had ever seen up to that time. Its armies had gone everywhere and this city on the Tiber had become the conqueror of all lands and peoples. Out from the capital of the empire the roads ran like the spokes of a wheel from the hub, and the soldiers marched forth from this centre to subdue countries and to hold them wherever the emperor wished to send them. Here was power which all eyes could see and which all men could feel. Over against this visible power, Paul knew that he had discovered a new kind of power. It could not be seen as armies could be seen, but it changed lives and

it remade cities and it upheld and supported
men and women in the hardest suffering and
trial.   Here was this man now bound with
chains, guarded by soldiers, a prisoner of the
emperor's, weak, frail, alone, but in reality
the bravest, strongest, most powerful man in
the whole empire.   Nero is dead now.   His
empire has passed away.   But Paul is still a
mighty power in the world.   Eight million
copies of his letters are sold every year.
Everybody reads what he wrote and he still
goes on working in the world as though he
were yet alive and speaking.

At first, when he came to Rome, he was
treated kindly and was allowed to have his
own house, though of course he was under the
care of Roman soldiers.   The guard was
changed every day so that he constantly had
new soldiers by him.   It gave him a splendid
chance to preach his gospel to the Roman
army, for he would surely never let a soldier
stay all day by him without telling him of

Christ. It must have *worked,* too, for, in his letter to the church at Philippi, he writes that "the saints in Cæsar's househould send greetings," and he also says that he has been able to spread the news of Christ through the whole prætorian guard. Perhaps he did more as a prisoner than he could have done as a travelling preacher. Paul was the kind of man that would appeal to soldiers. They could see at once that he was as brave as they were, and they could feel that he was in his way a hero, and they were ready to listen to his story and we may be sure that many of them went back to Cæsar's palace changed into "saints." Others went out with the army and carried the truth about Christ into the lands where they were stationed. "It has all happened right," Paul wrote to his friends. "My chains have helped to spread the gospel!"

During the first part of the time in Rome, Paul expected to be freed. He thought his trial would come off favourably, and he was

full of hope.   In this early period he wrote
a beautiful letter to his friend Philemon, who
lived in Asia.   He told this friend that he
expected soon to be free and he playfully
added you can get me a lodging, for I shall
be coming to Asia before long.   He had
found in Rome a run-away slave that belonged
to Philemon.   He had told the slave, who was
named Onesimus, about Christ and Onesimus
had become a follower of Christ.   Paul sent
him back to his master, changed from a slave
to a brother and Paul calls him his "own son
in Christ."   This was the way Paul's gospel
worked for all kinds of people.   It made
them new men, and it gave them a new rela-
tionship to everybody.   One day a poor, mean
slave, the next day a brother and a son!   In
this letter Paul calls himself an old man.   He
writes: "I am Paul the aged."   He could
not have been very old in years—probably not
more than fifty-five—but his years in prison
and the terrible hardships, through which he

had been, had left their mark upon him and he seemed old before he was old.

As time went on, and Paul had had two years in "his own hired house," he seems to have been taken to some imperial prison, perhaps to the famous Mamertine prison, which was deep underground, and very dark, cold and damp. It became more and more evident that the wonderful prisoner was not to go free again. His friends in Philippi remembered him and sent one of their number all the way to Rome to comfort him and to carry to him the things he needed in his hard prison life. He was very deeply touched by their love and kindness and he wrote an extraordinary letter of thanks to his first Christian believers in Europe—those men of Macedonia who called him to them. He told them that he did not know whether the outcome of his trial was to be life or death, but that he was "ready" for either event that might come. "I have learned" he wrote, "how to be contented with what comes to me. I know how to be successful and how to be defeated. I know how to be happy when I am full and I know how to be happy when I am hungry. I can do everything with Christ's help." "I want you," he told his friends, "to learn the secret. I want you to rejoice and again to *rejoice,* and evermore to REJOICE."

What happened at last, we do not know. Nobody has written for us any "We-Narrative" about the last prison days and about the trial in Cæsar's court. Some people think that the great prisoner got his freedom and went on for many years doing missionary work across the world, travelling with Timothy and Titus and the other helpers, and preaching in new lands and in new cities. But I do not think so. I think that he never left Rome again. The Jews who were opposed to him had a very strong case against him. They could prove that in almost every city in the empire where Paul had been there had been riots and uprisings and they could make it seem that Paul was the cause of these things. He was one lone man with a whole multitude of furious enemies and in Cæsar's court the testimony against him would count for very much, and would weigh very heavily. It seems most likely that the trial ended with a decision against the great missionary. If he was condemned, as I believe he was, then he was soon after executed, and, as a Roman citizen, he would be put to death with the sword. That is the steady tradition in Rome that he was taken out to the place now called the Three Fountains and there beheaded. We shall probably never know any more about the end of our hero's life.

One great fragment of a letter has been preserved for us. It does not tell anything about the prison, or the trial, or the manner of the death. But it does tell about his courage, his calmness, his faith and his noble spirit. It is a letter to Timothy, his young friend, written by "Paul the aged." It says: "I am already being offered up now, and the time of my departure is come. I have fought the good fight. I have finished my course. I have kept the faith. Henceforth there is laid up for me a crown of righteousness." At the end, as always through his life, he was "ready." Unmoved and undefeated, and, we may be sure, with his face shining, as Stephen's shone that memorable day in Paul's youth, he went to meet his death. They could kill his body with their sharp sword, but they could not crush his spirit or conquer his faith and hope. When his eyes could no longer see Rome with its capitol and its coliseum, he could see his Christ, and when his ears could not hear the shouting and the cries of the people, he could hear a gentle voice say: "Well done, good and faithful servant, enter into the joy of thy Lord." The hero got home with God at last.

PRINTED IN THE UNITED STATES OF AMERICA

www.ingramcontent.com/pod-product-compliance
Lightning Source LLC
Chambersburg PA
CBHW021056090426
42738CB00006B/370